The Price of Love

Nikola T. James

The Price of Love

Sidgwick & Jackson

First published 2007 by Sidgwick & Jackson
an imprint of Pan Macmillan Ltd
Pan Macmillan, 20 New Wharf Road, London N1 9RR
Basingstoke and Oxford
Associated companies throughout the world
www.panmacmillan.com

ISBN 978-0-283-07048-8 (HB)
ISBN 978-0-283-07056-3 (TPB)

1 3 5 7 9 8 6 4 2

A CIP catalogue record for this book is available from
the British Library.

Typeset by Intype London Ltd
Printed and bound in Great Britain by
Mackays of Chatham plc, Chatham, Kent

Acknowledgements

I'd like to thank the following people:

Myself for meditating so well and finding my agent Robert Smith, who is so wonderful and talented that he in turn found my editor Ingrid Connell at Pan Macmillan who has charmingly and supportively enabled this new author to deliver. My husband Connor, my rock, my soulmate, who has encouraged, helped and supported me always. Katrina, Jack and Mikaela, my wonderful children, who love and accept me for just who I am. We have laughed, cried, argued and cuddled. Love you lots. Thanks to Kev for looking after Kat. Special thanks to Mikaela for her help with word-processing and my technical ineptness; my brothers Harry, James and Joe who hold a special place in my heart. I hope you can let go of some of the past now as I have. Ian and Sue in Spain who held my hand while I scribbled, especially Sue who deserves a medal if only for having to put up with Ian's bad jokes. Pat, Helen, Ally, Ian, Sandra, the most loving, accepting and supportive friends I could ever wish for. Liz, my staunch friend and loyal supporter, and Philip who will probably never speak to me again. All my clients – past, present and future – from whom I have learned and am still learning so much about myself and about life.

Author's Note

In today's society, where people change career more than once in their working lives, it is no longer true to coin the phrase 'a job for life'. The only 'job for life' would seem to be that of a parent, which begins from the moment children are conceived and in real and emotional terms never ends.

Being a parent is the hardest job in the world, as well as the most rewarding. I make this statement as a parent myself and quantify it by adding, 'getting it right' makes it the hardest job in the world. It's also impossible, because we are only human and therefore are bound to make mistakes along the way. An underlying message in my book is that mistakes are okay. What's more import-ant is that our children know from the moment of conception that we love them for who they are, not for who we want them to be.

As you read my story you may feel that I blame my

parents' lack of love for the incidents that happened in my childhood. On the contrary, I know that both my parents loved me very much. The problems arose from their inability to communicate this well enough to make sure that first a baby, then a young child growing up felt safe, loved and accepted. The message that was filtered through into my belief system was: you are loved and lovable only 'if' you become the person we expect you to be.

Both my parents are now dead. I love them unconditionally but getting to that point has been a long road. I also have had to let go of the desire to make people into who I want them to be, rather than accepting them for who they are. My relationship with my mother was a prime example and it was never easy. The turning point for me came when I finally accepted, about twenty years ago, that she was never going to be the ideal mother I always wanted. Mum was just herself – exasperating and infuriating at times but also someone I learned to respect for who she was. From that point onwards we had a very good relationship.

My parents, like most parents – and I include myself in this group – did the best they could with the knowledge they had. Like life, parenting is a learning process, we're all learning on our feet.

Dad, Mum, love you lots, miss you.

The Price of Love

Prologue

THE FLASHBACK CAME FROM nowhere, or at least that is how it felt at the time. One moment I was standing in my kitchen, listening to my husband start his car and drive off to work, the next I was transported back almost forty years. I was once again in my first marriage, a prisoner, trapped by a man who enjoyed subjecting me to the most horrendous abuse.

Instantly I became overwhelmed with panic. I was shaking and sweating, my heart almost pounding out of my chest. Waves of sickness washed over me and my legs were like jelly. Then I felt 'he' was standing behind me at the sink. I could feel his hands all over me; hear him whispering in my ear. The next thing I knew I was curled up on the kitchen floor, my back against the cupboard. I was clutching my knees and crying. How could this be happening to me? I had worked so hard to keep 'the secret'. I was okay, wasn't I? A fully functioning adult –

well almost. I was good enough at most things I did. I wasn't perfect, but then who was? How could this stuff come leaking out now? It wasn't fair!

After the first flashback I resorted to learned behaviour, I did what my mother would have done and frantically cleaned the house for a couple of weeks. It didn't help – the flashbacks just kept coming. Neil was in my head again, inside my body, my skin crawling with revulsion. He was beating me with his belt, the raised studs drawing blood on my skin, telling me over and over how this was all my fault.

I felt frightened again and I wasn't sure what I could do. I knew I wasn't able to sit down cold and just talk about it – just say those words about the dreadful things that had happened. NO! NO! NO! my mind kept screaming as the words choked in my throat. I had given my husband, Connor, only the briefest details about this violent relationship in my past, telling him that the past was where I wanted it to stay. He respected my wishes and never questioned me further. And although the abuse I suffered represented the full catalogue – verbal, emotional, sexual, mental and physical – after forty years the only visible scars are the gashes on my stomach, which was repeatedly slashed with a razor blade. When the children were small and compared their tummies to mine, as children do, I would explain the scars away with excuses about pregnancy and childbirth and not taking care of my skin. I told the same thing to friends until eventually I almost believed my own version of the truth.

Although the scars on my body had healed and faded, they were still there. Every day, getting dressed or seeing myself naked in a mirror, I'd see them and for a second the memories would rise. But I had built a wall between my older self and the abused young woman and every day I pushed the memories back behind the wall: I couldn't allow myself to feel the pain from the past — I wouldn't allow it to spoil my life now.

I had been in therapy and dealt with the problems that sprang from my childhood, but these other secrets remained firmly locked inside me. I had never envisaged telling them to anyone, much less writing a book about them. But now I knew I would have to write it all down because I couldn't hold it in any longer. I decided that would be my therapy, remembering that as a trainee counsellor keeping a journal had been very cathartic.

Over a period of days it began to dawn on me that writing a journal maybe wasn't enough. If I was going to tell 'the secret' after all this time in the only way I felt I could, then I had to make it count — I would try and write a book. At first it wasn't so important that the book be published — it was for me, my family and friends; it gave me a voice. I hadn't realized how difficult it would be for those who love me to read about my secret life. It was particularly painful for my husband, who found it hard to cope with his feelings when he learned what I'd been through, but in the end it has helped my relationship with Connor grow.

Using my skills as a curative hypnotherapist, I was able to regress myself right back to the eighteen-year-old girl I once was when these traumatic experiences occurred. This makes the account much more accurate than just writing from a conscious memory. Under this self-hypnosis I heard every chilling word again, I felt the physical pain, I shook with fear, and re-experienced a kaleidoscope of other emotions. As my fingers typed at the computer keyboard I realized that the same inadequate words that my younger self used to describe her fear and emotions kept repeating themselves over and over again. I became aware of how emotionally immature I was then. As a child no-one ever asked me how I felt or if I needed anything – my life was all about how everyone else felt, and what they needed – and as a result I didn't have the vocabulary to articulate my own feelings.

I resisted the temptation to change the words in order to make reading the story more interesting. As a result it is written as it was perceived and in my language as a naïve teenager, giving the most authentic account possible.

My wish is that this book will help other victims and survivors, that it will give hope and encourage them to change their situations and start their own healing process. In the conclusion I have tried to explain how we can become trapped in abusive relationships. You may recognize your own circumstances there – I hope it will help you to accept that it is not you who is at fault. We are all very special people who deserve to be loved.

Chapter One

'WHAT KIND OF MAN hits a woman? None! No man hits a woman. You're not a man though, are you? Just a bully that's all you are. Call thi'sel a man, hit my lass will ya? Well come on then, hit *me*, see if *I*'ll let thee get away wi' it. Come on.'

That was my nana's strident voice, her Lancashire accent getting stronger as she grew more upset. In the background, my mum was sobbing and apologizing weakly for whatever imaginary offence had caused my father to hit her. My dad was shouting accusations, drunk and belligerent.

I was huddled next to my older brother on the stairs. We should have been in bed but had crept out to listen. This scene or one very like it was replayed many times during my childhood. The noise, the violence, would tie my stomach in knots of apprehension no matter how many times it happened.

★

I grew up in a small busy market town in a rural farming community. I have fond memories of it as a child, especially market day which was particularly exciting, with stalls selling fruit and vegetables, the myriad of different smells, the hustle and bustle of people going about their business with a sense of purpose, but always cheerful.

I was born in the late 1940s, a time when the nation was struggling to come to grips with the aftermath of the Second World War. My parents had had a typical war-time romance and had only known each other a short while when they got married. As my father was almost immediately sent abroad, they never really had a chance to settle down to married life and my mother continued to live with her parents for the duration of the war. My father, a tall handsome man, was from a large family. One of thirteen children he'd had a rough childhood and knew how to take care of himself in a fight. In spite of that he was quite intelligent and had passed his scholarship to grammar school, although he was unable to take up his place as his parents couldn't afford to buy the uniform. I don't think he and his brothers and sisters got to wear shoes very often. Apparently my paternal grandfather was an alcoholic so there are no prizes for guessing where the limited family funds were spent.

My mother, who was petite and very pretty, was an

only child, and very much a girl who never grew up. That's not to say she was spoilt – in many ways she had a difficult childhood too. Her mother, my nana, was a domineering woman who was not easy to live with. She liked a drink and would drop her ten-year-old daughter off at the cinema and disappear to the pub, completely forgetting to pick her child up again. On many evenings my mum would be left waiting at the cinema until gone 10 o'clock at night. She knew her parents' marriage was rocky and at one point both of them were having affairs. But whereas my dad's childhood made him tough, my mum's left her unable to shoulder adult responsibilities.

After the war my father found employment as a coach painter, but he became ill with a rare muscular disease and was unable to work for quite some time. With two children to feed – my older brother Harry and me – my parents struggled to make ends meet. For the first four and a half years of my life, our home was a prefabricated hut in a former wartime displaced persons' camp. My most vivid memories of the camp were the outside communal toilet block, and the horrible smell that hung around its vicinity. My dad had an enamel bucket in the house that he used to pee into during the day as otherwise, being the babysitter, a trip to the block would mean having to brave the cold and rain, dragging two young children with him. He used to sing 'I'm Forever Blowing

Bubbles' to camouflage the sound – a song that would be forever associated with him in my mind.

My mother had to go out potato picking and we would wait for her to come home with her share of the potatoes, plus a few bob, so that we could have chip butties (I love them even to this day). Dad used to shout at me because I was crying with hunger and my tummy was rumbling. I guess he felt awful and didn't know what to do to comfort me – we had no food until the 'potato winner' came home.

When I was four and a half we moved into a council house, part of a new estate. Now we had a real bathroom and an inside toilet and everything smelled so fresh and clean and new. The gardens at the back hadn't been laid out yet and were just earth, with a pile of concrete posts and some rolls of wire in the middle of our patch of soil. A couple of days later some workmen came and put the posts in-between the houses and fenced us in and we had our very own garden. It was wonderful.

Dad had started working again, so there was more money coming in, and things were looking up. Up to the age of five I remember my parents being very affectionate towards each other and my childhood being pretty normal. And then my nana moved in and everything changed.

She came to stay with us because she had broken her

ankle, and then never went back home. Before Nana arrived, the idea of her visit seemed quite exciting to me and Harry although my dad didn't want her to come at all – not even for six weeks. Mum pointed out she didn't have anywhere else to go – she was a widow with no other close family – and was unable to look after herself in the middle of winter. How would she cope with the icy conditions, the treacherous pavements, shopping with a broken ankle? Dad put up quite a verbal fight, pointing out all the horrible things she'd done to them when they'd lived with her for a short while during the war. She had made Mum do all the housework, had refused to give them a front door key, insisting they were home by 8 p.m. every evening, and turned all the lights out at 9 p.m. But Mum insisted – she always did what Nana told her – and in the end Dad had to give in to the pressure. After Nana arrived she cried a lot and Harry and I felt sorry for her. When we got to know her better we realized she could cry at the drop of a hat when bullying tactics failed her.

I don't really remember how she managed to take up permanent residence but she manipulated it somehow. There were fringe benefits though – she got a job once her ankle was healed so there was more money. She would buy me and Harry clothes and sweets, take us on day trips occasionally, help with housework, that kind of thing. Nana was quite nice to us children – it was my dad she couldn't stand, and the feeling was mutual. He always seemed to be in the pub after Nana came to live with us and there were rows all the time. I could never understand why she wasn't even just a little bit frightened of him. When she was horrible to him it used to make my toes curl with embarrassment and anxiety. There again, she was an old bugger but I liked her; she had balls.

She was also a big woman with a sense of humour who liked a drink. I remember she would sometimes come home drunk from the pub after a night out with her friends. We would hear her get out of the taxi and slam the door, stagger down the garden path while singing 'Danny Boy' at the top of her voice (she had a good voice too). She would bang on the door – too drunk to find the keyhole – and, when it was opened for her, virtually fall through it, fur coat hanging off one shoulder, hat all askew, still singing at the top of her voice, primed and ready for a row with my dad. The prelude to the rows always followed the same pattern: 'Right then, what's it going to be? Am I singing too loud, not loud enough? Am I too drunk, not drunk enough? What will it be tonight then?' My dad always obligingly took the bait.

★

Harry was already at school when we moved into the council house and six months later I started school myself. I think it was there I first became aware of the differences between us Council Estate kids and those from better areas of the town. Harry and I were always clean and tidy but I have a vivid memory of being asked by my teacher in infant school to stand on my chair. It was just after my birthday and I was wearing a new dress and my mother had put my hair in 'dinky curlers' after she had washed it the night before. I wouldn't stand on my chair at first because that's what the teacher made children do when they had been naughty. I tried very hard to be good all the time at school and now I was worried that I'd done something wrong. The teacher reassured me that she thought I looked very pretty in my nice new dress with my hair done up in curls and a matching ribbon. She just wanted the rest of the class to see how sweet I looked today. I was very relieved to hear this but it was embarrassing to stand on my chair while the rest of the class looked at me and clapped their hands. Although I was only six I think I felt that normally I must have looked a bit of a mess.

When I was about nine I made friends with a girl called Judith whose father owned a shop in town and I was invited to her home one Saturday to play and stay for tea. I couldn't believe that one house would have so many rooms, such a big kitchen. They ate their meals in a separate room, not even in the kitchen – and they ate real BUTTER. Judith had a bedroom to herself, so did her sister. I was totally blown away. As I left Judith's house that day I promised myself that one day I too would be rich and live in a house just like hers. I felt sad, I think it was because I had just begun to realize that some people are better off than others in more ways than one. The better-off people didn't include me. I knew I was different to them – grubby. I now recognize this feeling as second class. Although I wouldn't have known that then, it wasn't a good feeling.

For a long time Harry and I were the only children, but despite this we were never really close. On reflection, I think Harry was probably jealous of me. As often happens after the second child arrives, he didn't get as much attention as he would have liked. We were also subtly divided by my parents' different reactions to us. My mother thought the sun rose and set on Harry and he could do no wrong, whereas I was the apple of my father's eye, at least until I was eleven.

My father didn't think of Harry as a 'real boy' because he was a picky eater, quiet and shy, small for his age and not into sport or fighting. He was also not interested in doing well at school and failed his 11-plus exam. In an effort to make my brother into a 'real boy', Dad picked on him constantly and Mum spent all her time defending him.

Sunday lunch was a typical example, a meal the whole family dreaded. Harry hated vegetables and my mum always tried to give him the smallest portions possible. My dad would make her give him more, remarking that it was no wonder he looked so weedy and as if a puff of wind would blow him over. I remember sitting at the table with my tummy in knots willing Harry to eat as he forced down what to him was each nauseating mouthful. As a child who would eat anything, I couldn't really understand why he didn't like such a lot of foods. Nevertheless, I found the bullying and intimidation, the virtual force-feeding, quite frightening. By the end of lunch Harry, my mother and myself would be in tears. My father, however, would be pleased he'd won – again.

My mother seemed to resent the fact that my father wasn't constantly having a go at me. To be fair, I wasn't a picky eater, I worked hard at school and was more bubbly and extrovert than my brother. So while my mum liked it when other people said things like, 'no need to ask who your mother is, you look just like two peas in a pod', if people actually complimented me on some achievement or other she would always put me down. According to her I had 'far too much to say for myself'.

I was 'too big for my boots' and 'I needed bringing down a peg or two'. I guess it was because her own mother was very domineering and she always did what she was told. She thought little girls should be quiet and passive; I don't think I was.

And so, as children do, Harry and I both sought the love and approval of the parent we felt we had somehow disappointed.

Chapter Two

VISUAL HALLUCINATIONS WERE ONE of the side effects of the medication my father was taking for his muscular disease, and he gradually began to believe that my mother was having an affair. This psychosis usually focused on whoever was living next door at the time, but occasionally extended itself further afield. I remember she once took a job and he used to follow her around, trying to catch her out. He even took to sniffing her underwear to see if she'd had sex.

Unless my dad had been drinking, his accusations and the rows that ensued would be confined to within the family environment. Unfortunately when he drank (which he was not supposed to do, with the medication he was on), the results would be explosive. A few pints of beer would give him the impetus he needed to rush to the neighbour's house, banging on the doors and windows. He would shout obscenities and accusations through the letterbox and it would have been a brave man who would have faced my father in one of his drunken rages. Needless to say none ever did and it would be left to my mother to apologize the following day. She of course would always blame the drink: 'We don't want the neighbours knowing all of our business. It's bad enough that we're already a laughing stock and everybody's gossiping about us.' I wasn't really aware that we were being gossiped about until I was quite a bit older, probably in my teens.

All of this was very confusing for a child, and my father was very convincing – why wouldn't he be, he really believed he could actually see the affair happening! My mother strenuously denied all of the accusations (because, of course, they weren't true) and she often got a slap across the face from Dad for her trouble.

When my father, who was six feet tall, hit her – always after he had been drinking – he would only ever hit her once. My mother was a small woman and usually she would fall backwards into a chair and start crying and apologizing. That would be my nana's cue to give my dad a load of verbal abuse. She would accuse him of being a bully and tell him to pick on someone his own size. Sometimes, depending on how mad he was, my dad would give her a slap or a punch as well.

Harry and I would either be in bed listening to all of

this or on the stairs listening. There were often parties that we were allowed to stay up for, but these would always end up in a punch-up that Harry and I would be witness to. I can't speak for Harry but I found it very frightening and confusing. I never understood why my nana didn't just look after Mum instead of making things worse by goading Dad. It felt like she wanted him to hit her – to prove a point.

I remember having a conversation with my brother when he was aged about ten and asked me whom I believed. I said Dad, he said Mum. Unfortunately, it didn't take my brother long to run to Mum and tell her what I'd said – I got the strap from my mother for that.

My mother often used to hit me and Harry with a strap: Harry more than me to be honest, although he was her favourite. Most children were physically punished when I was a child and I don't think I was hit excessively but Harry certainly was. My dad only ever hit me twice. Once when I was nine or ten and Harry told him I had been showing the older boys my knickers. Not strictly true, I had been jumping from a tree onto a pile of grass and my skirt was being blown up by the wind and the force of jumping down. Harry was simply getting his own back on me because I had told on him for smoking – I was a terrible snitch. I'll never forget that day because I couldn't believe that my dad, who really loved me, was actually going to hurt me. He smacked my bare bottom; worse still, he actually laughed at the look of sheer disbelief on my face. I don't think he hit me very hard – he didn't need to, I was totally bereft.

When I was about nine my brother got into trouble with the police. He was small for his age and skinny, and was in a gang where the other boys were bigger than him. He was bullied quite a bit, but I don't think it would have been called that, back then. The gang broke into some property and, being the smallest, Harry was told to climb through the window. To cut a long story short, he got caught and the others got away. He was sent to a remand home for six weeks for an assessment because he said he'd had a blackout. On my brother's return home, and for about a year after (or at least that's how long it seemed), my father would come home from work and beat him with a riding crop, and make me watch.

I cannot begin to imagine what it was like for my brother physically – although emotionally I have a fair idea. For me it was absolute hell. I could feel my brother's pain and humiliation and I hated my father. I wanted it to stop; I wanted to make him stop but I couldn't. I was afraid; I was scared that if I did or said anything, he would turn on me. It used to make me feel sick. Dad used to give him 'six of the best' every night. Harry used to shout and cry and scream in the hope that the more noise he made the less whacks he would get but it never worked. His bottom and the tops of his legs were always red and bruised.

Despite everything that was happening within the family my relationship with my dad up until the age of eleven was warm and close. He wasn't the kind of father who sat and read stories or talked to his children. Day trips were not on the agenda, although Nana occasionally provided these. But I can remember the odd walk on a sunny day – after the pub shut and before it opened again. However, my usual treat was to be taken to the pub with my dad and plonked down with a glass of lemonade and maybe, if I was lucky, a bag of crisps – the ones with the little blue twist of salt – then ignored for two hours. I wasn't really bored though as I have always been a fascinated people-watcher. I noticed that my dad used to get more friendly with people after a couple of drinks, but after a lot of drinks sometimes he was nasty. It was always time to go home before I was fed up and the best bit was the taxi ride, because Dad had always had too much to drink to walk.

Some afternoons, when he came home from work, I would sit on Dad's knee and try to talk to him but I knew he wasn't really listening. He would go to sleep while I was chatting because he'd usually had a few pints.

Then I would kiss his cheek, which would be all stubbly (he had to shave twice a day), and he would smell of beer and cigarettes but I didn't mind that too much.

He was quite strict with me, especially as I got older, but at the same time he was more indulgent towards me than he was towards my brother. Boys had to be toughened up; little girls could be spoilt. I know he really loved me. I wonder if some of the emotional love that would have gone to my mother had my nana not come to live with us, was actually lavished on me instead. Maybe that was why my mum was jealous of my relationship with Dad, because she felt his emotional withdrawal from her. Even when he was having his delusional episodes and accusing my mother of having affairs, I was never frightened he would turn on me. He never involved us children in any of that. The target was always my mother and her so-called 'boyfriend'.

I would have loved to have felt closer to my mum. I remember pretending to be ill because it was the only time she gave me a cuddle. She wasn't a cuddly person really. Mum wasn't given to deep introspection but if she thought about her role as a parent at all she saw it as feeding and clothing us and keeping both us and our environment clean. In my adult years, as we became closer, she confided she wasn't keen on sex and implied that none of us would have been born if Dad hadn't practically raped her. I used to point out to her that this was quite a strong accusation. She would just say, 'You know what your father's like – nobody says no to your dad, do they? As far as he's concerned he's paid for his marriage lines and that's it.' As I got older I used to feel angry for Mum and try to get her to stand up for herself. Sometimes she would make a half-hearted effort but it never lasted long. A couple of slaps would usually put her back in her place.

I know she found me extremely difficult and I never really understood why. I tried very hard to please her but I never quite managed it somehow. If I cleaned the fire out I wouldn't have done it properly. If I dusted it wouldn't be good enough. If I washed the windows, they were streaky. I just felt like nothing was good enough – that *I* wasn't good enough – but that just made me try harder. Mum used to say I did things badly so that she wouldn't tell me to do them again, because I was lazy. I used to ask her to show me how to do them properly because I was only a child and I didn't know. She never would, she would just tell me to get on with it like she'd had to.

On the plus side, when she had some money she would buy me the nicest clothes she could afford. She came along to school for parents' evenings, concerts, sports days, those kinds of occasions which Dad never attended. I did appreciate her doing those things because I knew they were hard for her and she hated doing them. Mum felt, and was, totally out of her depth but she still turned up and made the effort. I feel really guilty that I used to hope she would turn up but dread it at the same time. Although clean, she was often shabby so that even as a young child I used to feel ashamed. Unfortunately, all the money she could afford went on clothing her children, very little on herself. And because she was very pretty, this somehow made me feel worse. I wonder now why my nana never bought her any clothes. My dad used to give Mum all his wages although he didn't make much money in his job in the hotel trade. However, he did make a lot of 'tips', but those were his 'beer money' – he was obviously doing well if his beer consumption was anything to go by.

When I was about eight the first of my two younger brothers arrived. James was born at home and my mum, who was in her late thirties by now, had a difficult birth. I remember playing outside and hearing her scream – scary stuff for a child. Then the midwife told me that she had found James under a gooseberry bush in the garden. I was cross with her because she obviously didn't realize I was almost nine and thought I was stupid. I'd been playing out in the garden all the time and she hadn't been out there once. So where did he really come from, I wanted to know. She started to tell me but my mum stopped her. Then James started crying and I never did find out.

After James was born Mum seemed to be up and about fairly quickly in spite of the 'size of the child'. I remember everyone remarking on how big, but also how beautiful, he was. At just under thirteen pounds in weight he seemed to fill his carrycot. He had the whitest of blond hair and the bluest eyes; he was adorable. I loved him instantly, but not so my dad who again accused my mother of having an affair with the fella next door. We had an extremely difficult few weeks until my dad decided to accept James as his own child and not a cuckoo in the nest. Lots of drinking went on during this time, and banging on the neighbour's door, shouting through the letterbox, rowing with Mum and Nana. Then I think he must have just run out of energy, burned himself out or something – he slept for a whole day and night and got up a completely different person; he made a big fuss of James, bought presents. It was unbelievable, how quickly and completely the change came about.

Standing in the garden just over two years later listening to Mum screaming when Joe was born seemed like the longest time imaginable. Even though at about nine pounds he was a more normal weight, Mum was that bit older still. I took her a cup of tea after the birth and she was so exhausted and shaking all over, I had to hold the cup for her while she drank from it. It was after Joe was born that she began to look older, gaunt – I thought she looked quite ill for some time afterwards.

Joe was a gorgeous baby with enormous blue-green eyes set off by the longest eyelashes I'd ever seen. He slept a lot and when he was awake seemed very happy with his own company, playing with his fingers and toes, a rattle or his pram toys, or watching what was happening around him.

I quite liked having babies in the house, somehow it made it seem special, but still I soon felt as though I had said goodbye to the small amount of childhood freedom I had been allowed. Now, as well as cleaning the house, I had to look after my brothers. My mum wasn't particularly maternal and none of her pregnancies were planned, but I don't think Dad was keen on condoms. My mum was Protestant and before they were married my dad was Catholic. Mum refused to change religion and there was a big family row with 'his lot' as Mum called them. Dad had to promise he would bring us up as Catholics. Apparently 'his lot' attended the wedding but weren't speaking to my mum or her family. They didn't speak until sometime near the end of the Second World War after my dad was wounded in the leg. Needless to say my dad gave up Catholicism when he took up Alcoholism and so we were brought up as Protestants. My mother sent us all to Sunday School though I'm fairly sure it was more to get us out of the house than because she cared about our religious education.

I was excited about my confirmation – I had a special white dress for the occasion and my mum had promised to come to the service. The day before, Mum had been 'back end', cleaning upstairs in the bedrooms. We had just had our lunch and as she wanted to go back upstairs to continue cleaning she told me to give Joe his bottle of milk. I was quite happy to do this because it meant Joe and I could have a bit of a cuddle – he was about seven months old at this time and such a cuddly boy. After he'd finished his bottle I changed his nappy and put him in his pram with his harness on. Normally he would have had a sleep but as he didn't look tired I sat him up for a bit to watch me dry the lunch dishes Nana was washing up.

The kitchen wasn't all that big so when I needed to put the cutlery away in the drawer I had to move the pram and, unthinking, I pushed it into the corner next to the cooker and the kettle. When I turned back from the cutlery drawer Joe was doing a macabre, contorted dance in his pram, his mouth wide open in a silent scream, his eyes full of unshed tears of pain and fear. My eyes took in what my mind could not accept. The flex of the now partially upturned and recently boiled kettle was entwined around his little hand and arm. Scalding water was spilling down him as he frantically tried to escape what must have been indescribable pain.

From somewhere deep inside me, in what felt like slow motion, I found a voice, not mine, a coward's feeble squawk. 'Nana – Joe, help him, help him please!' Everything happened in slow motion as my nana turned from the sink but couldn't see from where she was what had happened. It seemed to take forever for her to walk to the pram and remove Joe's arm from the flex of the kettle, shouting for my mother all the while.

When my mum arrived she started to shake and cry and went into shock. She couldn't even get back upstairs to get a clean sheet from the airing cupboard to wrap Joe in. I tried to do it quickly though my legs felt like lead and I had trouble finding a cot sheet. When I came back with it I was dispatched to ask the man who lived at the end of the road if he could take my mum and brother to hospital. He was the only person in our road who owned a car. I'm not sure how I even got there, my legs wouldn't move fast enough. I was crying and sobbing so much I don't know how they made sense of what I was saying.

My mum and Nana both went to the hospital and I stayed at home to take care of James. I'm not sure how

I got through the next few hours worrying whether Joe would live or die. I blamed myself for what had happened, wondering what my punishment would be, knowing that whatever it was I thoroughly deserved it. When Mum and Nana eventually got back the news wasn't good. Joe was in an extremely bad way and could possibly die. Apparently the next seventy-two hours were crucial.

Dad had been told and had taken himself off to the pub, while Mum turned her attention to Joe's pram and his discarded clothes. These had been stripped from him and thrown into the pram when the clean sheet was wrapped round him. She began washing his baby clothes in the kitchen sink in Lux soap flakes. I stood fascinated, watching her. She was talking about my confirmation the following day, telling me I wouldn't be able to go now.

'If you set foot inside a church, any church now, my girl, after what you have done to Joe, God will strike you down dead. You mark my words.'

I was frightened and shaking, tears rolling down my cheeks. So, this was my punishment. Would God really strike me down dead? I had no reason to doubt he would. As I watched her washing Joe's clothes, I noticed she kept pulling from his little cardigan and romper suit what looked like the skin off the top of the milk when it's just boiled. I asked her what it was.

'That's your brother's skin! You've done that to him, it's your fault he's in hospital fighting for his life and all you're interested in is going to church, being the centre of attention, getting confirmed. Well, it's not happening, madam, so forget it. That white dress is going back as well; you needn't think you're keeping that.'

'That's enough,' my nana growled from the doorway. 'Don't you think the lass feels bad enough? Stop putting old heads on young shoulders. We can't go tomorrow lass because we have to go to the hospital to be with Joe. Will you be able to go with Linda from down the road?'

I told her that I was sure that would be all right. 'But what if God does kill me?'

'I'm sure there's a few others more deserving of his attention first,' Nana replied.

As I lay in bed that night worrying about Joe and praying he would survive and get better I reflected on what Nana had said. I tried to take some comfort from her words but try as I might my mother's words were too strong and powerful for me to overcome. I slept very badly, dreaming of chariots of fire crashing through the roof of the church, avenging angels hurtling golden spears in the shape of crosses to strike me down as I stood on the steps leading to the altar; seeing myself mortally wounded, collapsed in a heap on the floor, the Archbishop shaking his head and pointing his finger at me exclaiming, 'Take heed, this is how God avenges all sinners!'

It was with great trepidation that I set off with Linda and her family for what should have been a proud and exciting day. Dad had just given me one of his looks, we had not spoken – there wasn't any need for him to say what he thought of me. Dad, Mum and Nana were going to see Joe, while James was staying with a neighbour until I returned (if I did).

The whole time I was in church I expected to be punished somehow. I don't really remember my actual confirmation or taking my first communion, it's all just a blur. I was just pleased to get out of the church in one piece. Everyone else seemed to be happy with their families. Linda and her parents were very kind to me but I guessed that was because they didn't know Joe's injuries were my fault, and that made me feel even more guilty.

I collected James and we amused each other as best we could until everyone returned from the hospital. Joe was holding his own, whatever that meant. The tension in the house was unbearable and I felt really bad all the time, my stomach churning with shame and fear. I think it was about a week before Joe was declared officially out of danger, and he stayed in hospital about three months. He had to have skin grafted from his little legs onto his arms and back.

After about a week my mum took me to see him. We had to wear masks and gowns so we didn't pass on germs. He was in a little room on his own, lying on his tummy, one arm bandaged up but his back uncovered. I took one look at it and I started to gag. I could feel the sick in my throat. His little back was just like raw liver and it was my fault. I couldn't look at his face I felt so guilty. I couldn't get my breath, I felt dizzy and sick. Blindly I groped for the door and somehow I managed to get outside into the corridor and pull the mask away from my mouth. A nurse in the corridor came rushing over asking me if I was all right. Mum, who had followed me out, said: 'Leave her it's the least she deserves after what she's done to her brother. It's her fault he's in here, she did this to him. She won't get away with it though. One day God will punish her, she'll have to suffer for what she's done.'

I started crying and my legs were shaking. The nurse, looking really shocked, put me gently into a chair. At the time I thought she looked shocked because of what I'd done; in retrospect I feel she was probably more horrified by Mum's outburst.

Who could know what Joe's personality would have been like had this dreadful accident not happened? When he came home from hospital he was very quiet and shy. He rarely cried and when he did he was a silent crier. His eyes would fill, sometimes the tears would splash down his little cheeks, but he rarely made a sound — as though all his pain and fear were locked right inside him and he couldn't let them go.

Chapter Three

THROUGHOUT MY CHILDHOOD I always had an underlying feeling of anxiety but I didn't really know what it was or how to explain it. I had no way of knowing that this was not 'normal' or 'natural' and nothing to measure it against. I always felt as though I was walking on eggshells, having to be careful of what I said or did in order not to upset either one or both of my parents.

We all felt it as children, even James, who was the most exuberant of us all. When he was seven he ran across the road and was almost knocked down by a car – a neighbour called by to tell my mum. Dad, who was also at home, was furious, saying, 'That boy needs to control his temper, what he's short of is a good hiding.' The women of the house all looked fearfully at each other. I can't speak for my mum and Nana but I certainly experienced a sick, gut-wrenching feeling and flashbacks of Harry being beaten in the kitchen.

Eventually, James came boldly marching into the house, almost defiantly I thought at the time as he came into the kitchen. Everyone started shouting at once and James began to look a bit scared. Dad shouted, 'Right James, what do you think you're doing running across the road in front of a car without looking and nearly getting yourself killed? Where have you been? Your mother's been worried sick about you.'

James went red in the face and denied he had nearly got run over. At this point Dad's temper got the better of him and he reached out for James, at the same time accusing him of lying. My brother's fear now turned to anger and he picked up a chair from round the kitchen table. I'm not sure if his intention was in the first instance to throw it at my dad or if it was to defend himself from him. However, he did throw it at my dad who was quite shocked at first but then just laughed. At the time it reminded me of when he had smacked my bare bottom. I think Dad laughed because he admired James's spirit. Here was a 'real boy', so in a way he was proud of him. Of course it didn't save James from a good hiding but I don't think he ever got another beating after that.

In spite of James standing up to my dad, showing he had spirit, his naturally cheerful and positive nature was eroded away as he moved through his childhood. The effect of my parents and his environment but especially the family relationships squashed him into the box of the third child in a dysfunctional family and everything that came with it.

Long before my tenth year I was well schooled in the art of keeping the family secrets. My father's problem both inside and outside of the family environment was always referred to as his drinking. The actual cause of the problem, that he was most probably struggling to come to terms with an extremely rare muscular disease and all that entailed, was never discussed. Knowing my father, he would have been feeling much less of a man, not able to take care of his family properly. And unable to talk about this (as a family we never ever talked about our feelings), he turned to drinking. The addition of alcohol to his medication turned it into a hallucinogenic cocktail affecting his emotions and behaviour. For us as a family, the knock-on effect of this was an emotional roller coaster that we learned to ride with varying degrees of trepidation.

As a young child, unaware of the underlying cause, I believed – because I was told explicitly by my mother and implicitly by what was happening around me – that Dad's drinking was our fault. I was terribly confused. I had picked up it was because Mum was being naughty and Nana was being nasty. However, Mum was saying, implying in other more subtle ways, that it was to do with us children too; that we had to be really well behaved and not upset Dad. I found this even more confusing and difficult. In order to keep Dad happy, I often had to upset Mum, as they both needed me to be someone totally different – my dad wanted me to be clever and ambitious, my mum just wanted me to help with the housework and look after the boys. Another example of what I have chosen to call Mum's verbal and emotional dyslexia was when I had my first period.

My menstrual cycle started very early, when I was ten years old. I awoke one morning to discover that I was bleeding to death, or so I thought. Sex education at that time didn't begin until about the age of thirteen or fourteen at school, and my mother had never told me anything about my own body and how it worked, or about sex and reproduction. She was probably more scared than I was at the time. Her only explanation to me, which was totally confusing and mystifying, was: 'This will happen every month now. Don't let boys touch you there! These are called sanitary towels; you need to change them about three times a day. If we run out, or if there's no money, you will have to wear these rags, like I have to.'

I didn't have a clue what was happening or what she was talking about. I couldn't ask anyone else because as far as I knew no one else had started their periods. It was about two years before I knew what it all actually meant. Unfortunately, it was not two years before boys touched me there.

At this very early age, while blindly trying to cope single-handedly with the problems and moods of puberty, I learned I had failed my 11-plus examination. I was devastated. A covered passageway ran between our house and the next-door neighbours' and I managed to make it home from school to there before the tears came. I sobbed, great racking sobs, and felt as though my heart was broken, my life in ruins. I didn't know if I could ever stop crying – why was I so stupid? I'd let myself down. Even worse, I'd let Dad down. How could I possibly tell him? Then I remembered the letter from school in my pocket. At least I'd be spared having to speak the words. Eventually I pulled myself together enough to try and sneak into the house. No such luck, Mum and Nana were in the kitchen making tea. Dad was in the sitting room in his favourite chair, napping – a euphemism for 'pissed and sleeping it off'. I sneaked in and put the letter on his lap and rushed to the toilet to continue crying. I couldn't hide for long though as my mother called me down to look after James while they finished making tea. She didn't even notice anything was wrong.

Mum called everyone to the table, and I felt sick

while I waited for Dad to join us. When he came through he didn't need to speak, as on many other occasions with Dad the look was enough. I immediately started sobbing again. Mum asked what on earth was the matter; at least now she'd noticed something was wrong, I thought.

Dad threw the letter onto my tea plate and ordered me to read it out loud. 'She's only gone and failed her 11-plus, the stupid little bitch. Thought you were the clever one, didn't you? Well, obviously you're not, are you? You must take after your mother after all. Better go and see if there are any jobs going behind the sweet counter at Woolworth's. That's where all the thickos go. At least you're not ugly as well. Better to be attractive and thick than ugly and thick, eh!'

Swallowing my tears I tried to tell Dad I had worked really hard and I couldn't understand why I hadn't passed.

'Don't bother, Nikola, you're just stupid. So it doesn't matter how hard you try – only first counts in this world, second's nowhere. Go on, get out of my sight, take that letter with you and read it. Get used to reading it and whatever the words say – just read failure and get used to it. That'll be your life now. One of the no-hopers – bottom of the heap. Still, you've always got your looks – just like your mother.'

My Mum and Nana had sat white-faced and silent through this tirade, not daring to interrupt my dad who was still half pissed. My nana put up her hand at this point and said, 'Let the lass finish her tea. She's done nowt wrong after all.'

Picking up baby James, who had started crying, and sheltering behind him for safety, Mum could be heard saying, 'She's only a girl anyway. What's the point in educating her, she's only going to get married and have children. And what's wrong with the sweet counter at Woolworth's? All the pretty girls work on the sweet counter.'

At this point my dad snatched the letter from me, tore it into shreds and stormed out of the house to the pub. When he got back from the pub drunk we all made sure we were in bed 'asleep'.

In the 1960s, if you didn't go to grammar school you were on the scrap heap. To me, going to grammar school represented a life of quiet academia, somewhere I could escape the stresses and strains of life at home and immerse myself in a world of books and learning. I would work hard and gain 'A' levels, and would be confident and strong. But my dreams and aspirations were now lost and gone, leaving a vacuum and emptiness in my very being.

My father's reaction was even worse than I could have predicted. On this dreadful day I lost the bond of closeness we had shared. I believed I had lost his love and protection, and that left me feeling totally isolated. This was reinforced almost daily by his perpetual verbal put-downs. He used to introduce me to his friends in the pub as his clever little girl but he now stopped doing that. When people compared me to my mum he would reinforce the comparison by saying, 'Yes, she is *just* like her mother.' Both of us knew he meant thick, and it was as though he had stuck a knife in my heart.

I was no longer allowed to sit on Dad's knee and chatter away to him while he pretended to listen then fall asleep. He would push me away, tell me I was too old for that now and to go and help my mother. 'Go and learn something useful, baking or cooking. You'll have to know how to do all those things, seeing how you haven't got much of a brain to rely on. How about hairdressing, you're easy on the eye, do you need qualifications for that?'

Dad had never spoken to me like that before. There was a coldness in the tone of his voice he had never used with me so far. I knew now that his love was conditional on me being clever, and because I had proved myself to be stupid I was now unlovable. My confidence and self-esteem plummeted into a big black hole; it drastically changed the way I perceived myself, and consequently how others perceived me. The change in my emotional chemistry, even at this young age, had an immediate and lasting effect, and made me a very easy target for the bullies at school who tapped into this vulnerability when selecting their next victim.

Chapter Four

I WASN'T LOOKING FORWARD TO beginning the new term at secondary school. The school had earned itself a bad reputation, and when I arrived there it turned out to be even worse than I had imagined. I had moved from a primary school with less than a hundred pupils to a secondary modern of about one thousand pupils. Apart from us first years, all wandering around looking a bit lost and out of place, the rest of the students appeared to be loud, pushy and raucous, and in general the contempt and distinct lack of respect between pupils and teachers was mutual.

The school curriculum was well short of being academic: no 'O' or 'A' levels, and languages weren't even taught. Punishment was by caning in the main, and there was no distinction made between whether it was a boy or girl who was at the receiving end. Perversely, being caned was almost like receiving 'brownie points'. Small misdemeanours meant hands and legs were smacked with a ruler. Pupils were hit on the head with books, or had blackboard erasers thrown at them. I don't think anyone ever retaliated by hitting the teachers back; physical punishment was just part of life for children of my generation.

However, I was never punished at school – I was too busy getting my head down and working. School was always an escape from what was happening at home. Sadly, Harry always seemed to be in trouble. After lunch one afternoon in Religious Education my form had just settled itself into our seats when Harry (whose form room it actually was) came wandering in with the cane. Mr Gloucester, the RE teacher and Harry's form master, made a big speech about this being an example to us first years of the kind of pupil we should *not* turn into.

I was sitting near the front of the class feeling sick and very anxious. My stomach was in knots as Mr Gloucester ordered Harry to hold out his hand. He hit him six times with great gusto. Harry didn't even change expression. I, on the other hand, was severely traumatized. This incident brought back to me the way Dad had beaten Harry after he got into trouble with the police, the way he still did punish him on occasions. Tears were running down my cheeks and I looked up at Mr Gloucester with utter contempt and loathing as he remarked, 'You can look at me like that young lady, but if it stops you from turning into a cheeky, lazy, ignorant lout like your brother then it's worth it.' Believe me, it wasn't worth it.

A lot of bullying and sexual abuse went on at the school. I'm almost sure the teachers were unaware of it, and no one ever 'grassed' to the teachers about what had happened to them. Certainly I never did, as I was threatened with what the consequences would be if I did.

Like most of the other students, I was vaguely aware that 'stuff' happened in the bike sheds, which were situated on the lower floor of a large two-storey wing, and were actually a garage-cum-bike shed. On the same level were the sports hall, the boys' and girls' changing rooms and showers, the music room and a cloakroom. I never allowed my mind to formulate what 'stuff' actually meant. I remember hearing bits of conversations from the older girls like:

'. . . Trapped there with three of them . . .'

'. . . Hand up my skirt . . .'

'. . . Broke my bra strap . . .'

I was in this strange jungle environment, my curvaceous body belying the fact that I was only eleven years old. I was a child with a naive mind in a woman's body, lacking the experience or understanding that would have helped me to defend myself against the attention of the older boys at the school.

The first time 'stuff' happened to me, however, was not at school. I had been working on a school project with my friend Rebecca. We had been to the town library and were making our way home together, as we lived fairly close to each other. Our mid-evening walk home took us past a coffee bar, which was a popular meeting place for the older teenagers and youths of the town. A little further on we were caught up by two older boys from school who fell into step with us. I knew them by sight, and they were about the same age as my older brother.

I suppose hormones must have been stirring somewhere, as I liked one of them and thought he was quite good-looking. The other boy asked me if I was Harry's kid sister, and wanted to know where we had been. A silly banter between us ensued and by the time we had filled them in on our riotous night out, we had reached a local short cut, a badly lit back alley. I automatically turned into the back alley but Rebecca continued along the high street. I called after her but she just shouted back for me to hurry up, as she didn't have all night. I was about to turn around and follow her, when the boy I liked draped his arm around my shoulders, and there was a gentle pressure for me to continue along the short cut. The other boy moved up on my other side. I hardly noticed, being too busy wondering aloud why Rebecca hadn't taken the short cut, as it would save at least ten minutes off the walk home and it was a freezing night.

Having had no experience with boys and now being alone with two of them, I momentarily felt quite uneasy, but I suppose I was flattered that two older boys would even pay attention to me. Besides they were being nice to me, and I had a kind of excited feeling in my tummy. About halfway down the alleyway, the boys stopped and the one I liked pulled me towards him and kissed me full on the mouth. This was the first time I had been kissed by a boy. It felt sort of soft but tingly, and he tasted of chewing gum and tobacco. I wanted him to kiss me again and he obviously realized this and did so, quite passionately. I found myself really liking this kissing 'stuff'. I was so engrossed in it that I didn't object at all when he suggested that we move over to the wall where it would be more private. Neither did it occur to me to wonder where the other boy had gone. I soon found out, however, when instead of leaning against a wall, I found myself pushed against the other boy by my passionate kisser. I screamed in shock, as I hadn't realized he was there, and immediately a hand was clamped over my mouth. I vaguely heard someone say, 'You needn't start to play hard to get now, when it was obvious you were up for it.' I remember thinking, 'Up for what, what does this mean, what does he mean?' I was quite scared now, and just wanted to get away.

A muffled struggle followed that lasted a few minutes, during which time the hand remained clamped firmly over my mouth. Eventually, I was wrestled to the ground. I was in complete panic and wondering if they were going to kill me. I didn't understand: what had I done? I was wearing my school uniform mackintosh over a dress, socks and shoes. The second boy had managed to undo the buttons of my mac and pull my knickers down while the other one pulled my legs apart and knelt between them, forcing his fingers inside me. The pain was incredible and I tried to scream and struggle. They both told me to shut up and be still. The second boy's hand was now over my nose as well as my mouth. I could hardly breathe and I thought I was going to die.

In this fear and panic I remembered my mother's words: 'Don't let boys touch you there.' These words kept going round and round in my head. I was now firmly pinned down by the second boy, and my energy was fading. The other one had moved away from my body and I heard him say, 'She's creaming her knickers, hold her still, I've got it out.'

What is he talking about? What does it all mean? What's happening? I was in such a panic, now completely aware something bad was about to happen to me, and I just couldn't let it. I had to get away. I must, I must. I summoned energy from somewhere deep inside me. I kicked, I lashed out, I threw myself about, and somehow, I don't know how, I got free. Fear lent me wings, as I ran away with their threats ringing in my ears.

I told my mum I had dropped my coat in the mud, and I got a clip round the ear for that. The incident had made me late getting home so I wasn't allowed to go to the library again that term. By the end of that week the boys' (possibly very much elaborated) account of what had happened that night had gone around the school like wildfire and my reputation had been well and truly established; 'gagging for it', I think, was one expression.

I was extremely frightened by this experience but didn't feel I could talk to anyone about what had happened. Rebecca was furious because she'd had to walk home alone. She somehow got it into her head that the meeting was not accidental. She told me we should be going out with boys our own age, but after my experience I totally disagreed with her: we shouldn't be going out with boys at all, ever.

I knew there was no point in talking to Mum or my nana. There was absolutely no one I could talk to. I was very confused about what had happened or what had almost happened. Although I had started my periods when I was ten and my breasts were well developed, I knew absolutely nothing about sex or even my own body. Instinctively, however, I knew that what had happened was wrong, even though I didn't understand what the boys had been trying to do to me, or why. Later that week at school some of the older girls, feeling somewhat miffed and jealous about my new unfounded reputation, cornered me in the toilets. One particularly flat-chested girl said, 'Just because you have big tits and a good body you're still just a stupid little first year and don't get ideas above your station.'

I was aware of being watched from a distance by these boys who on the surface appeared to be carrying on as usual. Sometimes at break time I'd be sitting on the grass with a friend and see them looking over, egging each other on, pushing and elbowing, shouting taunts. I would just ignore them.

Their hangers-on were a different matter entirely. They would sit on the grass, try to look down the front of my school blouse, grab hold of my breasts and other things too unsavoury to mention. Some of their suggestions were totally incomprehensible to me and one boy even asked me how much it was for sex. I still wasn't quite sure what sex was but I was beginning to get the definite impression it came under the heading of 'stuff' so I slapped him. He was totally nonplussed. 'What is it? Do you just do it 'cause you like it? You don't want to be paid for it? What's your problem, you tart? I'll have you for this,' he swore as he stomped off.

I found all this very confusing; it made me feel angry inside. The injustice of it – anyone would think I'd done something wrong, or asked for it to happen, or enjoyed it, or even wanted it to happen again. It was so frustrating and bewildering. I mean, was it my fault? Was it something about me that had made it happen? Did I ask for it? Did I deserve it?

I started cutting clumps out of my hair a few weeks after this. I would cut the middle out of my fringe or one of the sides, anything to make myself look unattractive.

A few months after the attack I had been to a lunchtime audition for the school choir. The music room, as previously described, was located near the bike sheds. The fact that I had been accepted into the school choir had put me on a bit of a high, otherwise I don't think I would have stopped anywhere near to the entrance of the underground garage/bike sheds to carefully put my music sheets in my school satchel. Oblivious to events around me, I was just fastening the buckle when the boy who had kissed me appeared from nowhere right in front of me. Since that horrible wintry night I had become aware of his reputation in the hierarchy of the school thugs and bullies. I froze to the spot facing him as he blocked my way. His arms were folded, and he was chewing gum while staring at me. It took my breath away and I was paralysed with fear.

'Told you we'd get you eventually, didn't I, you little slag?'

I heard sniggering from behind me and, to my horror, when I turned round there were another three boys from his gang. During this distraction, I felt my satchel being snatched from me, and my original attacker ran away with it. Not thinking of what might happen, and desperate to retrieve my satchel, I ran after him straight into the bike sheds.

Within seconds there was almost a repeat of the first attack, only this time I was no match for four boys. A hand was over my mouth, my skirt was up round my waist and rapidly my school navy blue knickers were pulled down. My head spinning, I heard one of them shout in total disgust, 'Fuck it, it's rag week, that's the job fucked.' Momentarily, I felt their vice-like grips ease, and I thought: 'Thank God for that, whatever he means. Must be something to do with my period.' I thought they were going to let me go – 'just let me go, please' – as I struggled and squirmed, trying to make my escape.

'No, I've told you, that one's mine! Take that rag off and turn her over. She'll have to take it up the arse, she's not getting away again. Hold her over that car.'

I did struggle at first, but there was no point after a while; they were too big, too strong. I thought the rapist had stuck a red-hot poker inside my bottom, I only felt it twice, then I think I must have passed out. When I came round I was all alone. I was all wet and sticky with blood and other 'stuff'. Eventually, I managed to get myself into the nearby girls' changing rooms. I had a shower, although I had no soap. I found a dirty towel in the lost property box to dry myself with.

I examined my clothes: knickers okay, not torn just dirty, that's okay. Skirt just a bit creased – that's good, no one will ever know. My bottom hurt, a lot, and I was bleeding. I was worried I might bleed to death and wished I could ask someone. I was scared, in pain but too shocked to cry. I desperately tried to hold myself together while thoughts churned in my head: was it my fault? Did I do something? It must be the way I look.

My first priority was to destroy the evidence because I felt so ashamed. Having managed to clean up and get my clothes sorted out and back on, I walked out of the changing rooms and headed for home. Although in pain, I suppose the trauma of this incident had dulled my senses. As I trudged home, my mind encountered my second priority, as I began to struggle with the problem of what I would tell my mother. Feeling confused, ashamed and dirty, I had a vague idea of how she would react if I told her the truth. I decided the only thing I could say was that I had really bad period pains. I felt very alone, and although my mother was oblivious to what had happened earlier, she gave me a hot water bottle for my tummy, which was very comforting.

Returning to school two days later feeling very frightened, I was then reprimanded for having left the school at lunchtime to go home without first informing my teacher and seeking permission. I couldn't say anything in my defence. Bearing in mind I was not yet twelve years old, the rape was a dreadful secret to keep to myself. Had I reported it at school no one would have believed me, and the retribution that may have followed, along with the shame, scared the living daylights out of me.

From time to time after this attack I bled from my bottom, and I continued the habit of cutting clumps out of my hair to such an extent that my mother would take me to the hairdresser and get it cut really short. I also used to pick the skin off the bottom of my feet until they bled, and some days I could hardly walk.

After my first year at secondary school the boys and girls were separated into two different buildings with separate playgrounds and sports facilities. The boys who had been involved in my sexual abuse had all been in their last year at school. They left to find their own place in the pecking order outside of the school system. The girls-only school environment was much better for me. I didn't have to worry about who I would meet around the corner, in the cloakroom or downstairs near the music room.

Unfortunately my reputation once established was never quite relinquished. I had boyfriends, but mostly for very short times. Once they realized that rumour lied and I wasn't 'up for it' they quickly moved on to some other girl who was. Of course they all felt it incumbent upon themselves to enhance their own reputation and mine by saying that 'they had', even though 'they hadn't'. When I used to hear these stories I would be impotent with fury but I soon learned that tackling the boy concerned got me exactly nowhere, except to make me feel even more angry and powerless.

Chapter Five

KEEPING SILENT ABOUT MY rape and the fear that it may happen again caught up with me at the age of fifteen, when I had some kind of nervous breakdown.

In my fourth year at school I had been made a prefect which was quite a privilege and I was very proud of this achievement. Amongst our responsibilities we had to be available to help younger students, do playground duty and make sure students were outside in break times. This meant going and looking in all the toilets, cloakrooms and classrooms and the garage/bicycle shed. At first this didn't bother me but after a while I became reluctant to enter the underground part of the school.

Then, one day, for the first time ever, I forgot my games kit. I told the games mistress I couldn't do games because I had started my period and I was in pain. I didn't have a note from my mother (naturally, because it was a lie) and the teacher was really annoyed with me for some reason. I'm not sure why, but she dressed me down in front of the class. She said that since I'd been made a prefect I had become smug and conceited, that I walked around the school as though I owned it and I needed bringing down a peg or two. So, she decided, I could spend my games period picking up litter.

I felt unbearably hurt and upset. I didn't think I'd been any of the things she had accused me of. I had been proud to have been chosen, but that was all right wasn't it? Still there must be something in what she said: my mum always claimed I needed bringing down a peg or two. I cried all the way home because I was so upset. Mum asked me if I'd been behaving like 'a bit of a madam'. I said I didn't think I had. She didn't believe me and my dad, who would have stuck up for me once, just looked at me and shook his head.

I was at an all-time low – I felt useless, stupid and a waste of space. Dad was on night duty that night and after he had gone to work I took a big handful of his pills. I wanted to go to sleep and never wake up. Unfortunately I passed out on the toilet before I could get into bed. Mum found me and managed to get out of me what I'd done. She kept forcing me to drink salt water to make me sick and took me into her bed. I spent all night in and out of consciousness, with terrible stomach cramps, diarrhoea and sickness. She wouldn't get a doctor because she said it was against the law to try and kill yourself and the police would send me to jail.

After a few days I recovered physically but I was still an emotional wreck. Now, on top of everything else, I had the police to worry about. I couldn't rely on my mum to keep quiet. At least, that's how I felt at the time. Actually, on this occasion I could, because as far as I know she never, ever told anyone. Probably if my dad had found out she would have got the blame.

A week later I went back to school but I was increasingly jumpy and definitely making excuses not to go into the bike sheds now. Then my paternal grandmother died. Mum and Dad were going to the funeral and would be away for a week. I begged to go with them, desperately needing to get away for a while. No, they said, I had to stay at home to help Nana with my younger brothers. I cried and begged and pleaded but to no avail, I definitely was not going.

Then I got angry, because I was frightened. The day they left I had a flashback outside the music room. I thought I was going to faint – I couldn't breathe. At the time I didn't know it was a flashback, I thought I was going mad. I just wanted to get out of there, I needed to escape. But it is obvious to me today that I could no longer face revisiting the scene of my rape and humiliation, not even one more time.

That night I lay in bed worrying about school, scenes from my rape flashing into my head. I was angry with my parents for leaving me at home when I could have escaped with them. I don't really know how it happened. I was certainly very desperate and I guess I found a child's solution to the problem: if I can't walk I can't go to school, ergo I can't walk.

It was as though I had built a wall between fantasy and reality. For a while Nikola was choosing to have a rest in fantasy where other people would take care of her. Certainly, when I got out of bed the next morning and my legs wouldn't support me I didn't think, 'Yeah good acting, well done Nikola' but rather, 'Thank God for that, at least I won't have to go to school today and face all that.'

A few days later I was in hospital with doctors sticking pins in my legs, asking me if I could feel anything. My answer would invariably be, 'Feel what?' My nana was worried about me but tried not to show it. However, Mum and Dad didn't think my mysterious illness was important enough to cut their visit short. When they did come home they brought an aunt and uncle with them who came to see me in hospital before they went back home. They didn't leave until they'd all got drunk and had a punch-up – I don't think they spoke for about twelve months after that occasion, which was not unusual for my dad's family.

Eventually the doctors decided there wasn't anything physically wrong with me and that I'd had a sort of hysterical paralysis. I started having physiotherapy and within about a week my legs were back to normal. My mind had come back to reality and nothing had changed. I needed some help to sort out myself and my emotions but we didn't talk about such things in our family.

I did get to see a psychiatrist, though, and I told him about the assault in the alleyway the night I had been to the library. He spoke to my mother on her own, presumably about what I had told him and how it was affecting me. Her way of dealing with any unpleasant crisis was to deny to herself and others that it ever happened. So, possibly because of the scandal and shame the incident would cause should it come out, she told him I was lying, and that I lied all the time. She told me never to tell my dad.

I really believed then that the attacks were my fault; it was something about me, who I was, how I looked. My self-esteem was getting lower and lower. The psychiatrist must have believed something of what I said, because I got a medical discharge and left school three months early. In retrospect, I believe one of the things I learned from my childhood was that however badly behaved the men in your life are, as a woman somehow you're to blame. Even if you think you're not, you still take responsibility for their behaviour and 'keep the secrets'.

My dad was always really strict with me and as I grew older he became even stricter. In the days before the pill it was a big scandal if girls had to get married because they were pregnant. Even after I left school I had to be in by eleven, which meant leaving the local dances before they finished. At the time that seemed really unfair and one particular night I disobeyed Dad and got home at midnight. He was furious and waiting up for me. I was prepared for a row but he just ordered me to go to bed which was probably just as well because I'd had a couple of babychams and was tipsy.

The following day, he didn't ask for an explanation, but simply informed me I wasn't allowed out the following Saturday. I instantly came back at him with, 'That's okay I wasn't going out 'till Sunday anyway.' I was in the kitchen, standing at the pantry door, drying my hands on a towel. He came up behind me and said, 'You can stay in all next weekend then, you cheeky madam.' Then he rabbit-punched me on the back of the neck.

I clutched onto the towel rail for support as my vision blurred. I felt as though I was going to pass out but by a supreme effort of will, or at least that's how it felt at the time, I didn't lose consciousness. Because I was older and more rebellious I hated him at that moment. He really hurt me, my eyes were watering from the force of the punch but I forced the tears back down past the lump in my throat. I was determined not to let him see me cry. Later, I cried not only from the pain of the blow but for the loss of my dad. How could what had once been so warm and loving and protective have become so cold and lonely and isolating? I could only conclude that somehow it was my own fault, because I was stupid and a big disappointment. Why did I always get everything wrong?

Chapter Six

I T WAS TWO WEEKS before my sixteenth birthday and I don't remember being particularly bored that day as I stacked shelves with bottles of Heinz Tomato Sauce. I was probably sunk in a reverie. Like most survivors of abuse I would often escape into a world of my own, where good always overcame evil, men were white knights in shining armour who loved me and wanted to take care of me, asking nothing in return – not forgetting of course, that the road to happiness was paved with gold and good intentions. Whatever, I was definitely not 'in the moment' that afternoon in the small grocery store where I worked for the princely sum of £2. 13s. 6d. a week.

When I think back now I am reminded of being about nine or ten at junior school during silent reading time. Often I would slowly become aware that the rest of my class were standing while I was still sitting, reading, so engrossed in my book that the headmistress's entrance into the room had not impinged upon my consciousness; nor had the entire class wishing her good morning, or the rather sarcastic conversation between my teacher and the headmistress about my lack of attention and bad manners. Nothing disturbed my concentration once I could escape into my imagination through whatever avenue was open to me at the time. Eventually, I suppose the change in the atmosphere in the room must have nudged me into a realization that something was happening.

So it was that afternoon. Although I was still daydreaming and automatically dusting and stacking, almost imperceptibly I became aware that the door to the shop had opened and closed, quietly but firmly. The manager, Geoffrey Green, came through from the back. He was young to be a manager, tall and very thin and bony, with short, dark, curly hair, a big hooked nose and sticky-out ears. He lived in a nearby village and also helped run the family bakery.

Although he was only in his mid-twenties, I think he struggled to know how to relate to women, especially young girls like me. When I had applied for the job he wanted to know why I had left school three months early and I had told him I'd been sexually assaulted. I expect that made him feel even more uncomfortable. He wasn't very assertive and as a result he sometimes came over as being a bit abrupt and sharp, but he was okay to work for as long as you did your job and didn't flirt!

Geoffrey began to talk to the newcomer and it was obvious he knew him quite well. Although I couldn't really hear what was said, it was a blokey, matey, up-beat kind of conversation. Even so, there was a subtle change in the atmosphere in the room; what had been calm and peaceful began to feel tense and charged.

Then this disembodied voice began to speak – I couldn't tell you what the words were because of the conflicting emotions within me and the physical sensations I felt all at the same time. The hairs on the back of my neck stood up, my spine went rigid with shock, my legs felt shaky, my heart was pounding and I felt sick and scared, then incredibly sexy. I had a very real feeling of danger but also excitement.

Eventually I became aware that the voices were moving into the office in the back and Geoffrey was asking for tea, although I think by the irritation in his voice he must have had to ask at least twice. I made the task last as long as possible in the small kitchen upstairs, washing and drying the tea cups slowly, and was just pouring boiling water on the leaves in the pot when I felt weird again. My spine got pins and needles right down its length, I was having trouble with my breathing, my Adam's apple was Adam's apple was too big for my throat

— I sensed I was being watched, but there was no sound. It was quiet, too quiet. I took a deep, shaky breath, swallowed, and turned around. ·

The newcomer was leaning nonchalantly against the doorjamb — his eyes were the bluest and the coldest I have ever seen. You could drown in those eyes and he would never throw you a lifeline, I remember thinking. It was a strange thought, especially for someone so young. Perhaps it was a premonition.

He was tall, about five feet eleven inches, with a muscular build and dark brown hair. I noticed how smartly dressed he was: suit, shirt, tie, short overcoat, shoes nicely polished. He had this intense way of looking, it wasn't staring, but when his deep blue eyes focused on you it felt as if he could see into your mind, that you couldn't hide anything from him. So, he was looking, not staring, but he'd certainly know me next time he saw me.

He explained that he'd been sent for the tea as it was taking so long — Geoffrey was serving a customer. The timbre of his voice was pitched quite low and his manners were impeccable. He carried the tray, opened doors for me. He had his tea and left after about half an hour although I could feel him watching me through the office window the whole time I continued stacking shelves and serving customers.

Maybe it was because we were alone in the shop and

it was a quiet afternoon but Geoffrey was quite animated after his visitor had gone. Breaking his cardinal rule of never talking about anything that wasn't to do with work, and even throwing in a bit of gossip, he told me that Neil was nineteen and in one of the armed services; that his family came from the same village as him and that Neil was home on leave. His grandfather was a well-known local businessman – 'so pots of money there' – and his father's family lived in a small town about thirty miles away.

Unfortunately his father, who he'd been very close to, had died in a car accident when Neil was twelve years old. Naturally Neil had been devastated. Apparently he was very like his father both in looks and personality and Geoffrey seemed to think that Neil had still not really come to terms with his father's death.

Apparently Neil had a sort of love/hate relationship with his mother who he adored but couldn't get on with. Her relationship with his dad had been very abusive, because his dad had an unpredictable temper and had been very violent towards her, sometimes in front of Neil and his two younger sisters. The marriage wasn't happy, Geoffrey said, and the car accident was a relief for Neil's mother. However, because Neil was so much like his father he was a constant reminder to her of what had been. Subsequently they rowed all the time because in her eyes he could never get anything right and as soon as he could after he had finished school Neil left home.

Geoffrey had gone on to explain that Neil never really said all that much but that their mothers were good friends and confided in each other. Then he laughed and added, 'And villages are small places you know, lots of curtain twitchers. What we don't know you can be sure we just make up!'

When I asked him how Neil coped with it all he referred to one or two 'womanizing episodes'. For some reason girls found Neil very attractive but he never stayed with any one particular girl for very long. Geoffrey said it was because he was too picky, looking for 'Miss Perfect', still he was only young. I remember thinking when he said this that Neil wouldn't be interested in me then. Not quite sixteen, I was already 'damaged goods'. My heart sank. Still, for what was left of the afternoon, I couldn't get him out of my head.

It was almost dark when I left work at 5.30 p.m. The grocery store was at the back of the high street. I turned right out of the shop doorway, walked about thirty yards, then turned right again down a short narrow alleyway onto the high street. There were quite a few lorries and cars on the road and I stopped at a fishmonger's on the corner, next to a Currys, and waited to cross the road.

Opposite there was a coffee bar and another grocer's shop with a doorway set well back.

As I waited to cross the road I got that prickly sensation you sometimes get when you know you are being watched. It was mixed up with all the feelings I'd had earlier in the afternoon and I felt like I'd been punched in the stomach. I looked around. There were people hurrying along the street, probably like me going home for their evening meal and to their families, but I couldn't see anyone watching me.

The lights changed and I crossed the street. Then I saw him. Standing far back in the grocer's doorway. Dark suit, dark coat, collar turned up. Watching, just watching me. He didn't speak but he half smiled. I felt like my body was on fire. I was scared. Or was it excited?

He was there every night that week. He never spoke, he never came into the shop again, but every night when I went home from work he was in that doorway. Then one night the doorway was empty and I felt bereft.

I didn't see him again for two years.

Chapter Seven

RUMOURS, GOSSIP AND SCANDAL-MONGERING are rife in small towns anywhere in the world. In the early Sixties I guess it was a sign of the times that, because I left school three months early, everyone assumed I must be pregnant. When there were no signs of a pregnancy the abortion theory came about pretty quickly, also the miscarriage in mysterious circumstances. Needless to say, these Chinese whispers did nothing for my reputation and at times the unfairness and injustice of it all, in view of the harsh reality of what had actually happened, was more than I could bear.

My self-esteem sank lower. When other people are down on you, it's hard not to take responsibility for that on board, even when you know you are blameless. In spite of everything, over the next two years my natural, bubbly personality began to reassert itself. I had always been cheerful and outgoing, no matter how bad things were at home – and they usually were pretty bad. Appearing happy was our cover for keeping secrets.

I changed jobs three times over the next two years, from the grocer's to a shoe shop, to a greetings card shop, then to a hotel as a receptionist. You could do that in the Sixties, leave a job one day and walk into another the next. I liked the hotel receptionist's job; it was varied, had a measure of responsibility and I learned to type in a limited way, so I settled into that and kind of breathed a sigh of relief. Even my dad let up on me a bit. Anything was better than shop work in his opinion.

In the meantime my emotional life was in turmoil. At home my parents continued to fight, using me and my two younger brothers like emotional punchbags. Harry, my older brother, had left home as soon as humanly possible, going straight from school into the army. He had chosen a regiment that was stationed at the opposite end of the country to where we lived. After he'd left, a lot of my time and energy was spent wondering how I too could effect my own escape plan, although the situation seemed pretty hopeless as I had no qualifications and no money. We were still poor, so board and lodgings at home took virtually all my wages. Out of my first wage packet of £2. 13s. 6d, board and lodgings came to £2.00. I could have just run away, but I guess that although I was desperate, I wasn't quite desperate enough. In retrospect I wish I had taken action.

Then I met George, destined to become fiancé number one. I was almost seventeen, he was in his mid-twenties. He worked in a family-owned business in town, and he was tall, dark and I thought handsome in a roguish sort of way.

The thing about George, when I think back, is that he looked like what he was: a gambler. I just didn't recognize it at the time. He would not have been out of place in a cowboy movie, sitting round a table in a wild west saloon, dealing cards and slipping the odd one out of the cuff of his sleeve.

The thing about me is, I don't actually agree with gambling. So when I found out that the reason his cash flow was so erratic was because he bet all his wages on the horses – indeed, that's where my expensive engagement ring had come from – the ring went back and he was sent packing.

It wasn't quite as heartless as it seems. At the time I was devastated as I did believe I was in love with him. Our relationship wasn't sexual, but that wasn't unheard of at that particular time. I was very confused about what love was, but felt that there should have been a spark between us, something which was missing. Of course I was also far too young to get married, but George was very upset and couldn't understand my problem with his gambling. To be honest I think we both had a lucky escape.

Losing George was harder because I didn't have many friends really. Because of my so-called 'reputation', women were wary of me and didn't want me around their boyfriends or husbands and men thought I was an easy lay. This was compounded by the way I looked, my personality and an air of knowing sensuality which was totally unconscious on my part.

It was through a friend from school that I met fiancé number two, Andrew. He was gorgeous and a really sweet guy. By trade a forester, he was very strong and fit, as well as being good-looking, intelligent and a genuinely nice person. At the time I really thought he was the one. The spark was definitely there and I did love him as much as I was capable of loving anyone.

One night, about a month after we had become engaged, we went out for a drink to one of the popular bars in town, one of those olde worlde places with inglenook fireplaces. I was on my way back from the ladies' toilet when, as I walked through the crowded bar, I suddenly felt as though I'd been punched in the stomach. Andrew was standing sideways on, pint in hand, laughing his head off and chatting away to someone who was standing with his back to me, tall, slim, dark-haired.

He was laughing too. I felt hot and then icily cold. I remember giving myself a good talking-to – oh for heaven's sake, what on earth's the matter with you, he's only a bloke for Christ's sake. It probably isn't even him, lots of people look similar from the back. That kind of talking-to.

But it was him.

Andrew introduced me and Neil was extremely polite and pleasant, never letting on that we had met before. He bought us a drink and told amusing stories about life in the armed services at home and abroad. It turned out that he had a girlfriend, whom he talked about a lot, and before he left he arranged to meet us for a foursome the following weekend.

After he'd gone Andrew told me he'd known Neil for years. They were schoolmates at one time, although he hadn't seen him for ages because he'd been abroad.

I felt as though I'd been thrown in a bag and shaken up. I certainly didn't want to go out with Neil and his girlfriend. Danger signals were going off all over the place and I wanted to stay as far away from him as possible. He was trouble, I just knew it. I was repelled but attracted at the same time.

And so Andrew and I had one of those stupid squabbles – not a row, it was too childish for that. It descended into the 'we always go out with your friends, never with mine' rubbish. I lost and we met up with Neil and his girlfriend the next weekend. It was a strange night. I thought Neil and his girlfriend Sheena must have had a row, because she was chatty with everyone else but didn't say much to him. Andrew told me she was fine and I was just imagining it. What would he know? He was too busy hero-worshipping at the feet of the Master to even notice whether I was there or not. I did think that Sheena was very touchy-feely with Andrew, probably because she and Neil had fallen out.

Neil, on the other hand, spent a lot of time just looking at me – not staring, just looking. It made me feel very uncomfortable, hot and prickly, cold and icy, panicky, sick – oh, and lots of other things all at the same time. I asked him why he was doing it and he just said, 'Because I can. Why, does it bother you?'

When I told him it did a bit, he just shrugged his shoulders and went to get the drinks. Afterwards Andrew said Sheena had been coming on to him all night and a few weeks later we heard they had split up.

I soon had problems of my own. Having found my ideal mate I now discovered I didn't want him anymore. I was so screwed up, because of what had happened to me at school and because of my childhood, that I wasn't really capable of having a relationship with anyone. Andrew was loving, decent and kind – and somehow our relationship was too nice, too sweet and sugary. At home I was used to rows, shouting, tension, angst, and never being able to relax. With Andrew I knew exactly where I was: the centre of his universe. He treated me as though I was fragile, breakable – of course I was but I didn't know it. I became bored. Everything was too predictable.

Our relationship went through an 'on–off' period, then a 'push him away – miss him – reel him back in' period. In spite of my best efforts to make Andrew behave badly, he continued being noble and nice. I wanted to finish it and be able to blame him, but in the end I told him I'd cheated on him and that was the end of our engagement. I was broken-hearted but relieved.

I was extremely mixed up and confused after I broke up with Andrew. We moved in the same social circle, so we saw each other all the time and it was obvious we were both hurting. It was worse for him – he couldn't understand why, or what he had done wrong. I knew he hadn't done anything wrong – the problem was that he had done everything right and I didn't deserve him. He was too good for me, he just wasn't aware of it yet. But one day, if we had stayed together, something would have happened and he would have seen me for who I really was. Then he would have dropped me like a hot potato. It was better for it to happen now when I was in control.

How much worse to be rejected and abandoned further down the line when it would hurt even more and maybe I would never get over it. Better for him to maybe always love me a little bit than one day realize I was just trash and hate me. That's how little I thought of myself.

About eight weeks after I split with Andrew, Neil called me at work and asked me out. I felt very strange about the invitation. Part of me was surprised, but on some level deep inside I recognized the inevitability of us having some kind of relationship. Although I don't think I could ever, in my worst nightmare, have envisaged the sheer horror of what that relationship would be.

But he did. He chose me very carefully.

For our first date Neil and I met up in the late afternoon and went for a walk, then a drink and a meal. We talked a lot, in fact we talked non-stop, but I can scarcely remember any of the content of that conversation. In retrospect I realize that is not unusual. Although Neil was incredibly witty and charming he actually told me very little of a factual or personal nature about himself. Most of our conversation, certainly before our marriage, centred around me and my life. What I do remember is an intense feeling of sensuality between us, and underneath a sparking electricity that felt dangerous and feral. I was drawn to it like a moth to a flame.

He walked me home and we arranged to meet the following day. Then he kissed me goodnight. That was the first time he had ever touched me and the experience was beyond words. A rush of feelings, like a great secret that had been stored inside me, now came spilling out. His mouth was warm and real, he made me feel drunk with desire. We were both left gasping and laughing with what felt like relief. Something had happened to me, something had clicked, as though a switch had been flicked, and I felt as though I had come home.

For me, the next six weeks were a roller coaster of emotions. I had never felt happier, more secure, more loved and lovable. Someone liked me just for myself. They found me interesting, intelligent, even funny. They wanted to spend all their time with me.

By now I was eighteen years old and my previous relationships, because I had been sexually abused, had either been 'pure' or consisted of me offering my body – my 'gift of love' – in the guise of sex. Neil never discussed sex before marriage with me; kissing and cuddling was as far as we went. I didn't miss having sex – not that we were completely chaste. Neil had this way of loving me with his eyes; he could sit next to me in the car, or beside me in a chair, and his hand would lightly touch my waist, stray over my hip or slide along the upper curve of my buttock, almost imperceptibly touch my nipple. He would kiss my fingers or brush the hair from my face as all my senses slowed down. His fingers would comb through my hair and onto my neck as he told me how beautiful I was. We would share the same breath as we kissed and I was totally lost in space and time. Then he would talk to me until I had a sexual climax – sounds weird I know, but it wasn't 'talking dirty'. He would tell me how he was going to make love to me when it did happen but he would say it romantically and sensuously, with great eloquence.

After a whirlwind six-week romance, Neil asked me to marry him and I said yes. I was in love (again) – I was certainly in lust – and I was being treated with respect. I was also desperate to escape from my home situation and there didn't seem to be any other way of doing that except by getting married – not that I thought of my motivations in that way at the time. I truly felt I had found my knight in shining armour. This time I would 'live happily ever after'.

How wrong about everything can a person be?

Chapter Eight

NEIL WAS BEING POSTED abroad soon and wanted to get married in six weeks' time.

'What's the hurry?' I said. 'You're only going to be away six months.'

But he seemed to think if we were married I could go with him or we could get married quarters somewhere. I didn't think it was possible to arrange a wedding in six weeks, especially as my parents had no money to pay for it.

'No problem,' he said, 'leave it all to me. It will be the most memorable day of your life!'

So he arranged everything, paid for everything, chose everything, even my dress and the bridesmaids' dresses.

I was swept up by his enthusiasm but the run-up to the wedding wasn't all a bed of roses. His mother was not happy. In fact most of his family were distinctly unhappy, apart from his paternal grandparents and aunts and uncles.

I had a bit of a run-in with his mother and her boyfriend who came to see me one evening when Neil was back at camp. We were in the sitting room, drinking tea and making awkward small talk when Neil's mum finally came out with what was bothering her. She was quite naturally concerned about how quickly things had happened and so was her partner. The emphasis throughout the conversation, which I thought was quite odd at the time, was that I didn't really know him – not that we didn't really know each other. Even my mother, not the brightest button in the box, picked up on this, bless her.

'You don't know what you're letting yourself in for, Nikola,' Neil's mum said. 'He's got a temper on him but I don't suppose you've seen that. He keeps it well hidden. Just last weekend he had a huge row with one of his sisters and he went for her, over something or other – nothing really. He'd got something into his head, like he does sometimes, and up he went like a volcano.'

My dad awakened from his drunken sleep, fixed her with a steely stare, and remarked, 'No one's perfect, but Neil's always behaved like a gentleman. He's polite, and he's obviously been well brought up. He and Nikola both seem to be very much in love. What's the point in putting problems where there are none? We're very pleased for both of them and hope they'll be happy together.'

Neil's mum, who by now was red in the face and

obviously embarrassed, blurted out, 'He's got no money you know.

Dad sat forward in his chair, his face white with temper. 'Are you suggesting what I think you're suggesting?'

While Neil's mum huffed, her partner stood up, saying to no one in particular, 'I can see this is getting us nowhere darling. Perhaps we had better leave.'

Whereupon my nana piped up, 'You're like me, lad, just an outsider. This is nowt to do with us, best we stay out of it.'

I was too embarrassed and ashamed to speak. I felt really hurt, clearly not good enough for her precious son. Did she really think I was marrying him because I thought he had money? She made me feel like a gold digger and tried to make Neil look like some kind of monster.

In retrospect I think she was trying to warn me about his behaviour without betraying him but at the time I was so besotted I couldn't see how much Neil was already in control of me and my life. So his mum and her partner got sent away with a flea in their collective ears and the wedding went ahead, just as Neil had planned it would.

★

Weather-wise it was the day from hell, pouring with rain that was whipped into our faces by the gale force winds. Some may have seen this as a bad omen but not me; I was floating around somewhere in the stratosphere and barely even noticed.

Neil's two sisters were already at the house when I arrived back from the hairdresser's. There were gasps of amazement all round as they saw that my shoulder-length hair was now much shorter and curly. Neil had requested the new look and I was only too happy to oblige. However, it had taken much longer than anticipated and we were now tight on time so I rushed upstairs to change.

There were clothes, shoes, bridesmaids large and small, and a pageboy, make-up, hairspray and conglomerate clutter all over the place. Julia, Neil's eldest sister, came to help me. As I flung my clothes in all directions she stood ready with the dress. This was no time for false modesty and naked I struggled into the bridal knickers and bra.

'My God, you're absolutely gorgeous,' Julia said. 'And not an ounce of fat on you. Why anybody could think you were pregnant, I have no idea!'

I was a bit taken aback by her honesty. She must have seen the shock on my face because she quickly consoled me by explaining that people must be thinking it because we had decided not to have a long engagement. 'Most people do – unless they are expecting a baby.' Well, that did take the edge off her remark, and I joked that they were all going to get a bit of a shock when they found out I wasn't pregnant and I really had married for love. We both had a laugh about that as I hurriedly finished getting ready.

There were a lot of people outside the church, even though the weather was foul. Presumably they came because they too thought I was pregnant. God knows what they made of the dress, chosen by Neil. For a start it was white. Well, you didn't wear white did you, especially if you were not a virgin, or if you were pregnant, had a past, a reputation, not in a small market town in England in the 1960's. I could hear the gossip mill starting up as I walked up the path to the church.

The ceremony was beautiful and I really enjoyed it, especially the exchanging of vows. The feeling between us was so special, and I was very happy. Even the sun came out for about fifteen minutes to allow us to take some photographs.

Neil had booked the best hotel in town for the reception and it was excellent. Everything went off without a hitch, although we realized later that my eldest brother wasn't in any of the photographs. Admittedly, Neil's mother and her boyfriend had faces like slapped arses all day, but everyone else seemed to enjoy themselves even if they didn't wholeheartedly agree with our marriage for whatever reason.

I was having such a good time that I didn't really want to leave the reception; I liked being the centre of attention. I couldn't believe it was time to go, but Neil said it was, so it must be. I went to change and before I knew it we had left the hotel and were on our way to Scotland for our honeymoon.

Although I come from what you could call a drinking family, I am not a consumer of large amounts of alcohol. I do drink, but only in moderation, and my capacity for alcohol is reduced to nil before about seven in the evening. If I drink before that time I find it very difficult to stay awake and usually end up with a horrendous headache, even after just one glass of wine.

Predictably, soon after getting into the car to go on honeymoon, I started to feel sleepy. Neil was saying something about me flirting with the best man, which I thought was silly, and about halfway through his monologue I fell asleep. I later woke up with a terrible headache which seemed really unfair given that I'd only had four or five drinks over the space of about four hours. I moaned to Neil while we stopped to get some headache tablets, hoping for sympathy. He was very quiet and I wondered if something was wrong, but decided to give the tablets time to work before I asked him, as I was feeling really rough. Then I fell asleep again.

The next time I awoke was at our first night's stopover on the way up to Scotland – our 'honeymoon hotel' I suppose you would call it. It was a quaint old-fashioned hotel-cum-pub/restaurant in a village. It was very comfortable and clean, and the staff were polite and friendly. It had been a long day, and I was certainly glad to get there. We were told the dining room would be closing soon, so we hurried upstairs to change, as we were both feeling a bit peckish.

Neil's moodiness was all about nothing really, or so I thought as I quickly changed into a dress. Neil looked at me. 'Not that one,' he said quietly.

'What?' It was said so quietly, I wasn't sure I'd heard him properly.

'I said, not that one.' His voice, although quiet, was cold as ice.

'Why not? I like this dress, what's wrong with it?' He had never criticized my clothes before.

'I don't like it and that means you won't be wearing it again. Put the green one on and hurry up, I'm hungry!' His voice sounded peculiar, like chipped ice.

I was absolutely taken aback; he had never spoken to me like that before. Ever. I was shocked, but then, seemingly from nowhere, anger surged up in me.

'Who the hell do you think you're talking to? Don't fucking tell me what dress to wear. This is my dress and I like it, and I'm bloody well wearing it, you cheeky bastard.'

I was so busy remembering the marital advice my mother had given me about starting how I meant to go on, and not being walked all over the way she had been, that, I swear to God, I just didn't see it coming. I did, however, feel it connect with my right eye – his fist, that is – and luckily for me, I landed in a chair.

Neil only ever hit me twice on the face in a temper, and this was the first time. I don't really remember feeling anything immediately afterwards, just numb, as he leaned over the chair with his face all screwed up and hissed at me, 'Clever girl, no supper for you now. You've obviously got a lot to learn about obedience and who's in control. That was your first lesson. I'll leave you to ponder on what the second lesson could possibly be.' Then he was gone.

I couldn't believe it; I was in shock. Who is this person? All over a dress. Where has this come from? What have I done wrong? How could I have managed, in the space of a few hours, to turn this lovely, charming, romantic man, my saviour, into a monster? Someone who would actually hit me because he didn't like the dress I was wearing. I must have had too much to drink at the reception. He did say something in the car about me flirting with the best man, but I wasn't being serious, it was just a bit of fun. I told him that. Then I slept all the way here, which must have been boring for him – he must be annoyed about that too. How can I put this right? It's all my fault; I've spoilt everything, and it's a total disaster.

This wasn't how I expected to spend my wedding night. Not that I was a stranger to men hitting their wives, having seen my dad give my mum or my grandmother a backhander enough times.

Being left on my own, I was frightened. I suppose my eye was sore because it was swollen, but I was in such a panic I couldn't really feel it. I was scared of what would happen when he came back, but what if he didn't come back? I didn't even know where we were (Neil said it was to be a surprise). It seemed like the hotel was in the middle of nowhere and I had very little money. I'd never been on my own before, anywhere! I didn't know what to do, so I did what my mother would have done and pretended it hadn't happened. I had a bath, unpacked, and got into bed, trying to keep calm and hoping that everything would be okay. I would just have to try harder, or be different, or something, I wasn't sure what. By the time I went to bed I'd convinced myself it had all been a misunderstanding.

Neil was away a very long time. I couldn't sleep — my muscles ached with tension, and my eye was throbbing. My head ached so much it felt as though it was splitting in two by the time I heard the door open and then close quietly behind my new husband. After visiting the bathroom he turned on the bedside light, and having retrieved the dress he did not like from the wardrobe where I had hung it earlier, he told me to put it on.

'But Neil. I'm in bed, Neil.' Even to me, my voice sounded like a nervous whine.

He grabbed me by the hair — no mean feat, now that it was short — and dragged me from the bed.

'Now you're not. Put it on *now* — no underwear, whores don't wear knickers.'

'What?' I gasped.

'Get on with it. You've really spoilt my day, and now you have to make it up to me. You also have to be punished so you know not to do it again. This is only for your own good, remember that. It's bloody tedious for me, I can tell you.'

The bed in the room was an old-fashioned four-poster, fairly high, a lot taller than a modern divan. He made me put a pillow on the edge of the mattress, lift up my own dress and, having unzipped his trousers, he made me position myself on the bed on my stomach. I then had to open my legs to the position he desired while he shagged me. He warned me not to cry, because it was only what I deserved; this was what happened to naughty, disobedient girls. They didn't deserve respect or anybody being good to them; they were just there to be used. After he had ejaculated he dragged me into the bathroom, took a razorblade, slit the dress from the top to the bottom and ripped it off me. He then made me wipe between my legs with it before he threw it in the bathroom bin.

I collapsed shaking on the bathroom floor while he ran a bath and chatted away just as though everything was normal. Except the content of the conversation was not normal for me at that time, although it very quickly became so. It was a critique of my appearance and behaviour; of how I had upset him and let him down. My hair was now too short because, even though he had gone to all the time and trouble to tell me exactly how he wanted me to have my hair, I couldn't be bothered to listen properly. So I'd had it cut to the length he had wanted it to be *after* it was permed, not *before* – this meant that now it was far too short, and not the exact length that *he* wanted it to be.

I must have done something to the dress he'd gone to all the time and trouble to pick out and pay for, because it didn't look *exactly* how it was supposed to look, how it had looked when I had originally tried it on. So, what had I done to the dress? Well, I'd had an underskirt made for it because I felt that the material was so delicate and fine that, without an underskirt, it was see-through. But he was furious and said that it was irrelevant whether you could see my legs or not. He wanted me to wear it without an underskirt; and if I loved him, really loved him, that's what I would have done.

Flirting with his best friend, his best man, all day — what was I, some kind of tart? What kind of woman does that? Why — supposedly for fun? He didn't think so; he had come to the conclusion that I had done it just to make him look stupid. Well who looks stupid now, with a black eye? He really hoped for both our sakes that I was a quick learner, because I really had ruined what was supposed to have been the happiest day of his life.

This catalogue of my misdemeanours went on and on, while we had a bath together and he put ice on my eye. Then he dried me with a towel, took me to bed and, with incredible finesse and great sensitivity, made the most fantastic love to me. I hated myself and my body for enjoying the experience, for having multiple orgasms and for choosing the black knight instead of the white knight.

When I woke up the next morning, I felt as though I had been drugged. Maybe that was to do with the shock, the adrenalin that had been surging through my body the previous night, lack of sleep, too much alcohol and no supper. I certainly wasn't feeling how I was expecting to; like Snow White awakened by her handsome prince. I felt more like Little Red Riding Hood, only this time the big bad wolf really did get her and eat her all up.

The fullness of my bladder ensured a speedy but stealthy exit from the marital bed. I've never been one to lock the bathroom door, so I was still sitting on the toilet when Neil came strolling into the bathroom and asked me if I remembered when I was learning to read at school. How first of all you read aloud and then, as you progress, you become a silent reader. I said yes I did, why?

This time I did see it coming. He reached out, it seemed to me in slow motion, and grabbed a fistful of my left breast, yanking me up off the toilet, all the time chatting away, always quiet, always controlled.

'You need to cultivate the art of being a silent screamer, darling. I really can't abide lots of noise, especially first thing in the morning, so sshh.' He put the index finger of his other hand over my lips. 'No noise, hmm. Now, who said you could leave my bed?' He raised his eyebrows and I took this as permission to speak.

'I needed the toilet – aah,' as he squeezed my breast.

'Answer the question, who said you could leave my bed?'

'No one.'

He squeezed and twisted the skin of my breast as he sighed patiently and explained that I'd got off to a bad start again today, hadn't I? I couldn't speak — I was in agony, plus I hadn't finished peeing when he yanked me off the loo, and it went all over the place.

He told me to clean up the mess and have a bath because we were having breakfast in our room. Thanks to my bad behaviour, we couldn't appear in the dining room, as I had a black eye and everyone would know he'd had to discipline me. Breakfast would be here in half an hour, and he hoped both the day and my behaviour were going to improve.

I was pleased to leave that hotel behind, although sunglasses in Scotland in October are not very convincing, I can assure you.

Chapter Nine

M Y MEMORIES OF THE rest of our honeymoon are a bit sketchy, probably because of the trauma of what happened on my wedding night. I was badly hurt physically, but emotionally the damage was much worse. The extent of the nightmare that was going to be my life was becoming more obvious, literally by the hour. I quickly learned that if there was to be any tenderness, any love, kind words or even conversation, they would all be instigated by Neil. He was in control of everything. I used to dream about a man being the centre of my universe, I have to admit, but this wasn't quite what I'd had in mind. It certainly wasn't the way I wanted it to be.

What I do remember is that we drove all over Scotland. Depending on what mood Neil was in, the days could, at least on the surface, be happy and carefree. But underneath was a constant thread of anxiety as I worried about what would happen next to change Mr Nice Guy into Mr Control. Sometimes the anxiety would rise to the surface as I would listen, feeling incredibly tense and charged, while Neil chatted amicably about my faults and failings and how we needed to work together to change them/me, because at the moment, let's face it, I was just a liability. He was always reminding me how much he loved me, and that he was going to all this trouble because he loved me. However, he only had a finite amount of patience and he did feel I was ungrateful and didn't appreciate the effort he was putting into the relationship. I said nothing in reply – I was speechless.

For the entire honeymoon I struggled to come to an understanding of who Neil really was. He didn't punch me again but the fading bruise around my eye was a constant reminder of what he was capable of.

On four or five occasions during our trip Neil left me in the car. His manners, as always, were impeccable – he would ensure I had been to the loo, had a bottle of coke to drink and something to read. Did I need the window open? Was I okay? Then he would lock all the doors and disappear for a couple of hours to buy me clothes. I wasn't allowed to go with him and I rarely liked anything he chose. He never bought cheap clothes, but they were revealing. Over the course of our marriage, with the exception of family occasions when he allowed me to wear the more sophisticated demure styles, I much preferred, Neil generally dressed me like a tart, and I hated it. So my appearance changed over the course of the honeymoon, as my wardrobe expanded. Each day he either told me what to wear, or laid the clothes on the bed, including underwear, shoes, tights, dress/trousers/jumper/blouse, coat, jewellery, make-up, nail varnish, perfume – everything.

On one occasion I did remark that the nail varnish he had chosen, a particularly virulent red, didn't match the colour of the dress I was meant to be wearing. His response was to flick the ash from his cigarette, casually lean over and stub it out on the back of my hand. He then remarked that the colour of the nail varnish was perhaps more suited to the burn on the back of my hand. As I stared at him, stupefied, he shook his head and said he couldn't understand why I had to learn everything the hard way. It was simple really; I just had to do as I was told. Then he walked into the bathroom and turned on the taps for his bath.

The pain was absolutely unbearable. I wanted to run my hand under the cold tap but he was in the bathroom so I couldn't. Instead, I stuck my head under the pillow and sobbed. I could hardly swallow for the lump in my throat; I felt as though I was choking. My heart was hurting so much I was sure it was breaking. He was supposed to love me; he said he loved me; so why did he keep hurting me? All I ever seemed to do was upset him, so was it my fault?

I was so confused. It wasn't that I made him angry, not after the first night. He was always patient and long-suffering, and I knew I was a disappointment to him. I suppose, in retrospect, that's also how my dad made me feel. Neil was cold. He could be a warm person on the surface, but underneath he was very cold. It was as though my pain and suffering had no impact on him whatsoever. I see that now. He wanted to punish me, needed to see me suffer, and he felt I deserved it. In a way it was necessary – he tortured me because it made him feel powerful, but also just out of interest, to see what would happen, how much I could take; and maybe because he was scared of losing me if he wasn't in control.

I soon learned to obey the rules. I don't like physical pain, and by the time we got back to my parents' house about twelve days later, I guess I knew my place.

The basic ground rules were:

Listen carefully to Neil's instructions and follow them to the letter.

Don't speak unless you are spoken to, or unless you have been given permission to speak.

Ask permission to go to bed and to get up.

Ask permission before getting out of bed to go to the toilet.

Each day, wear what you are told: clothes, shoes, make-up, jewellery – all chosen by Neil.

Eat and drink what and when you are told.

So, on the surface I was all bright and bubbly and full of myself, because that was how Neil told me to behave. Underneath was a different story. My scattered thoughts went round and round as I desperately tried to find a solution to the puzzle that was my husband, a way to make the relationship normal.

I realize now that Neil's story about us getting married quarters abroad or in this country at such short notice was most unlikely. He probably knew at the time that nothing would materialize, but he wanted me under his control before he disappeared abroad for six months. Maybe he was worried that Andrew and I would have rekindled our relationship if he wasn't on the scene.

During this time I only saw him at weekends, as he was away at camp during the week. At weekends we stayed mostly with my parents, and occasionally with his mother and sisters. So providing I obeyed the ground rules, things weren't too bad. Neil, because he was staying in someone's home, had to curb the darker side of his nature to a great extent. By the time he had to leave I had almost convinced myself the problems on our honeymoon had all been my fault.

But Neil made sure that our last night together was absolutely unforgettable in the most sensuously exquisite ways imaginable. He was warm and wonderful, kind and caring.

Nevertheless, I was relieved when he left the country and I knew I had a reprieve for six months. What I was not prepared for was my sense of utter desolation; I genuinely and desperately missed him.

Almost as soon as we began our relationship Neil had insisted that I leave my much-loved hotel receptionist job. The practicalities made sense to me at the time. It was both shift and weekend work and as Neil was in the Forces he was away all week so weekends were usually the only time we could spend together. I wasn't too keen on my new job – mainly accounts work in the office of an agricultural feed merchant – even though the salary was better.

There was a married man in the office who was sexually harassing me and although I was no stranger to that kind of situation I was totally naïve when it came to dealing with it. Before the wedding I had spoken to one of the married women in the office and she had remonstrated with him. But that had made it worse. At first he was furious and denied it, then his efforts intensified. When I approached this woman again she was not as sympathetic and I felt she either didn't want to get involved or he had convinced her I was lying.

I tried to avoid being alone with him but he usually managed to manipulate the rota so that two or three times a week we were in the office at the same time over the staggered lunch breaks. He was always creeping up behind me and pressing himself against me, or wedging me in corners, trying to kiss me, touching my breasts or my bottom. He kept telling me he loved me. Even I wasn't naïve enough to believe that. He made my flesh crawl.

So I wasn't really looking forward to going back to work after the honeymoon. When I started back that Monday morning there seemed to be a bit of an atmosphere. On the surface everyone was friendly and polite, then during the course of the day remarks were made about my work, about the fact that one or two mistakes had been made in the month end accounts. I was asked to see the owner of the company at five o'clock and spent the rest of the day worrying about what I'd done. Accounts aren't really my 'thing', but I am a careful and conscientious worker and whatever I am doing I always try to do it to the best of my ability. That's not to say I don't get things wrong, I do, and maybe because of the wedding and this guy at work I hadn't been concentrating properly.

In my five o'clock interview with the boss we had an interesting conversation during which he virtually accused me of having to get married because I was pregnant and obtaining the job under false pretences. I was extremely upset. I couldn't understand why he would think I was pregnant but he just kept insisting that there could be no other reason for the haste of the wedding. I kept protesting my innocence but he wouldn't believe me. In the end I apologized for any mistakes I had made and gave in my notice. He grudgingly said he would give me a good reference and advised me against accusing staff members of 'indecent acts' when my own morals were highly questionable. I informed him that the company's low opinion of me was now mutual and I would forgo my wages in lieu of notice as I didn't think we should subject each other to the indignity of sharing a workspace.

I was absolutely floored. After my experiences of the last few weeks this was the last thing I needed. The woman I confided in had obviously talked to the owner of the company and my protagonist. The owner clearly felt that after he had trained me I was going to leave him in the lurch because I was pregnant and in those days most women left work when they started a family. Well,

I suppose I *would* have been leaving him high and dry after six months, but not because I was pregnant. When Neil came back from his posting and was assigned his married quarters we could be sent anywhere, so I would have had to leave then anyway.

Once again I felt as though I had let myself down. My reputation was in tatters and I wanted to rail against that familiar feeling of unfairness and injustice. I knew that only time would tell and in time I would be vindicated, but I wanted everybody to know now – I didn't want the whispering campaign. If only the jungle telegraph had known they didn't have to resort to innuendo and half truths. The day-to-day reality of my life was much more scandalous and worth a good snigger than anything they could possibly have dreamt up in their vicious little minds.

I dreaded telling Neil. Thank God he was back at camp and I could call him on the telephone. My throat was all dry and scratchy and I could scarcely breathe as I concentrated on trying to stop my legs from shaking so that they didn't give way in the telephone box that night. It was probably a combination of cold and fear – it was a frosty night and I'd had to wait my turn, only about fifteen minutes but it felt like an hour. I remember the faint smell of urine as the door clanged shut behind me and I plonked my change down on the shelf beside the piece of paper with the phone number on. I took a few deep breaths to steady my nerves and with a shaky hand picked up the big black telephone receiver. My fingers shook so much I couldn't get them in the holes to dial the number and had to use my pen. It took me a couple of tries, but eventually the number connected and it began to ring. I was so frightened I thought I was going to pass out as I waited for him to pick up – it must have rung about seven or eight times before he answered.

I just couldn't speak. My mouth opened, but no sound came out. I swallowed hard as he asked who was there. I had to speak quickly or he would put the phone down. Then it would be worse. I gave myself a mental shake, shifted my centre of gravity from my head to my stomach somehow, and found my voice. I used it to do what any manipulative child would do to get herself out of trouble. I didn't exactly lie, I told a version of the truth. I could hear myself babbling on about being accused of being pregnant, giving in my notice, coming away with a good reference. Neil was absolutely fine with what had happened, or with what I told him. I don't think the possibility I would ever deceive him in any way, ever be anything but totally honest, occurred to him. All he said was that I should have asked his permission before doing it but he would let that go this time. After all he was going away soon and I would have to get used to making some decisions on my own. He decided against me having another job saying it may not be worth it just for the six months while he was posted abroad because we would most likely move after that.

Something kind of clicked way back in my head then. At the time I thought it was just relief that I'd got away with it – that there would be no repercussions. Later, I realized it was something totally different.

In our relatively short relationship Neil, with his extreme control, unpredictable use of violence and relentless chipping away at every facet of my sense of self-worth and usefulness, had surrounded me with a solid wall of fear. When he mentioned that he was going to be away for six months, and that I may occasionally have to make a decision on my own, I saw a small crack appear in this wall. My mind began to work overtime with plans for escape.

Still, I was lonely after Neil had gone and wrote him long, frantic letters. My situation felt worse because I was living with my parents, two younger brothers and grandmother, the very scenario I was originally so desperate to escape from. The fact that I didn't have a job compounded this. I would work in a bar occasionally and sometimes helped out a friend who was a hairdresser, shampooing when she was busy, but it became increasingly obvious that I needed to occupy my time.

Christmas, New Year, January and February passed *slowly* and I became increasingly bored, almost desperate. Now, when I look back, I'm not even sure if it was a conscious plan or a subconscious wish – maybe I've put my own interpretation on events after they happened – I just know that, somewhere in my head, the solution to my problem was beginning to take shape.

On a Sunday visit to Neil's mother I mentioned how bored I was. I knew she would empathize because she had worked all her life, even while her children were very young and when it wasn't 'fashionable' or socially acceptable to do so. I don't think she was particularly maternal. By that I don't mean to imply she didn't love her children, I know she did. Rather that she was a cool, withdrawn person who found it hard to show her feelings. Nevertheless, since the wedding, although neither of us would ever be friends we had reached an uneasy truce. I was relying on her being a supporter of the Protestant work ethic and she didn't let me down.

Her suggestion for relieving my boredom, as I guessed it would be, was that I took a job. I immediately confided that Neil didn't think it was worth it for the short time he was away. She beamed at me as she mentioned that, so long as I didn't mind being away from home for a few months, seasonal work would be the perfect solution. I couldn't quite meet her eyes as I confirmed that it was a brilliant idea and bemoaned the fact that I hadn't thought of it myself. I am not a good liar, especially not in a one-to-one situation — but I guess I must be better than I thought.

I felt really bad about manipulating Neil's mum like that but I was desperate. I had to get away; I would never have got my mother to agree to something like that unless Neil had suggested it first. She wouldn't willingly give up the extra money she got from me, or the help with the housework and looking after my brothers. I didn't think Neil would agree if it was my idea, but if he knew his mother had suggested it he would. Even though they didn't get on, he would do anything for her. I wrote to him immediately and so did his mum. His answer came back quickly in the affirmative.

I was free.

Chapter Ten

I FOUND A SEASONAL JOB as a waitress in a holiday town some distance away. The pay was lousy, the tips were good, the hours were long, the uniform atrocious, but guess what? I was nineteen years old, it was the first time I'd lived on my own, no one was there to control me, and I tasted freedom for the first time in my life. This small seaside town seemed to be practically the drugs capital of the world and I had already decided to seriously misbehave over the next few months. After all I didn't have anything to look forward to so I may as well make the time that I had really count.

When I arrived at the small family-owned hotel it was late afternoon and in spite of feeling physically tired, emotionally I was elated. I had escaped from everyone – Neil, my family, the gossips in my home town. I wondered if that was how caged birds felt when unexpectedly gaining their freedom, or even criminals on their release from prison. As I stood outside the hotel all of my senses seemed to be heightened. The foliage in the small garden wasn't just green, but vibrantly differing shades of dazzling emerald and dark moss; I noticed the subtle shading of the daffodils, from a harsher gold to a buttery yellow. The hotel itself wasn't just white and pink, it was brilliant white and soft, petal-pink like a rose. The glass in the windows really sparkled, reflecting the late afternoon sun. As I went through the doors my feet seemed to sink into the deep pink of the carpets and everything smelled fresh and clean with just a hint of lavender.

To the right was a small, curved wooden reception desk. It resembled a bar more than a reception area I thought, then realized it was indeed also a bar. Mr Jones the owner was busily polishing this curved piece of wood and as I approached I realized that the smell of lavender was emanating from this polish. He seemed pleased to see me, welcoming me warmly. He was a short, barrel of a man in his mid-fifties with a bald head and warm brown eyes. When we met at my interview I had liked him immediately; he seemed kind with a sense of humour, but also the type of bloke who wouldn't stand any nonsense. Now we had a bit of a chat about my journey, the weather and the duty rota. He then took me into the dining room and introduced me to a girl called Chrissie who was to take care of me. Promising to see me tomorrow he disappeared, muttering something under his breath about hoping I would get settled in okay.

Meeting Chrissie was a mind-blowing experience for me. She was folding napkins in the dining room and even in a black skirt and white shirt I could see she was a hippie. My first thought was, how on earth are we going to be able to communicate, I don't even speak the 'love and peace man' lingo. I didn't need to worry. Chrissie was great. We were total opposites in everything, but a devastating combination and, for a time, we became the best of friends. She was a student, small and very slim, boyish in fact; I was taller and very curvy. Chrissie's hair was very blonde, almost white, with frizzy curls halfway down her back and she had lightly tanned, freckled skin. My hair was light auburn and shoulder-length, my eyes blue, my skin creamy. She wore rings on every finger, loads of eye make-up, her hair was tied back with a leather shoelace and in no way was she beautiful. She wasn't even pretty to be honest, but there was something about Chrissie that acted like a magnet to me. She had energy, confidence, charisma and class.

In a perfectly modulated Oxford English accent she told me she worked on and off at the hotel when it was mutually convenient with the Jones's who were friends of her parents. Her accent didn't prepare me for the shock of discovering her hometown was in the North of

England. By the time she was finished folding napkins and straightening up the dining room I knew that her father was an officer in the navy, that she had travelled all over the world and lived in a few different countries. She had a younger sister, her mother was wonderful and really 'cool', and she was about to take her 'A' Levels before going on to train as a nurse. In short, she was everything I wanted to be and wasn't.

We set off for the 'staff accommodation' to give it its posh name. Really it was a converted garage with a corrugated iron roof, and in total contrast to the hotel it was a bit seedy to say the least. To the right as you went in the door was a bathroom with five toilets and three shower cubicles, three washbasins and one bath. The floor of the whole place was concrete throughout and on the left of the front door was a bedroom with a window that ran the length of the wall. It was set high up near the ceiling and was about eighteen inches wide. Through another door was a lounge containing a black and white television, an old, scratched coffee table on which perched a tin ash tray, and a three-piece mock leather suite that had definitely seen better days. The same size and type of windows were in here as in the first bedroom and also in the other four bedrooms so nowhere had much of a view. These four bedrooms – cupboards really, they were so small – all opened out onto the lounge and were furnished with single beds and chests of drawers. All in all it was not very salubrious and there was no heating – but somehow it didn't seem to matter. In any case I wasn't planning on spending much time there.

The rest of the seasonal staff hadn't arrived yet but Chrissie and I decided to hit the town anyway, on our own. After Neil had gone on his posting abroad, I had bought myself some dark hide-your-figure-away nondescript clothes, which felt good to me. I didn't want to draw attention to myself. But still, as we wandered into a bar that night I felt like a drab moth next to Chrissie, who was as colourful as a butterfly with her flowing hair, turquoise and gold floaty skirt, scarves, beads and earrings. It didn't matter that she wasn't pretty. Chrissie was smart and witty. She knew how to dress to make people notice her, but she only ever dressed for herself. She was in your face, but what she was saying was, 'This is me, if you like me that's great, if you don't that's okay too. I know that if you don't like me that doesn't mean it's because I'm not okay.'

When I joked to her that all the guys in the bar were eyeing her up she quickly retaliated. 'Look, in my opinion,' she said, 'and I don't know what your problem is, although you've obviously got one, but in my opinion you can do and wear what you like but what you can't do is hide that fantastic figure and that beautiful face.'

I feel it is important to point out here that we were probably both pretty merry by then. Well I would be having had more than two drinks! The great thing about our relationship was we were friends right from the start, we trusted and accepted each other. Yes, we loved each other.

We had a great night. Chrissie knew lots of people of both sexes, different cultures and classes. We drank a bit (not too much), we smoked dope (a joint, no more), we laughed all night, we cried a bit (not much), and we just had a fabulous time. I met some great people, one of whom I became quite close to over the next couple of months. But the important thing for me about that night was that I was in control. I chose when to go out, what to wear, who to go out with, who to speak to and when to go home.

This was freedom.

The following day three other girls arrived to make up the full complement of dining-room staff. Like me they were all from provincial towns and of a similar age.

Susan was about five feet three inches with long dark hair and blue eyes. She was a Scot and when she was angry or excited no one could understand a word she was saying, she used to talk so fast.

Jennifer was about five feet and a little bit and had

fair- to mousy-coloured hair pulled back into one long plait she could sit on. Her eyes were hazel and she had a deceptively quiet voice that belied her very dry sense of humour.

Then there was Catherine. She was about five feet seven with red curly hair and green eyes. She was big-boned, not fat just solid, and oh dear was she clumsy. That girl just had to look at something and it broke. She was also extremely sweet and kind, a bit naive and sometimes a bit slow I thought (although the truth turned out to be something different altogether).

Work was extremely hard and the hours were long, but it was an absolute hoot and it was good to be with young people all day. The other staff in the hotel were all middle-aged or older and seemed po-faced to us, making us even more determined to get as much fun as possible from the job. Everything was a laugh to us; we were just young and daft. The older members of staff kept reminding me that I should have more sense, and should be setting a good example. Although young, I was a married woman, tut tut! There were no complaints about our work – they seemed more concerned about our rather racy social life and what we got up to in our free time.

This was the summer of 1969, and the glorious swinging Sixties' revolution had finally seeped into this small tourist town. It didn't take me long to become intoxicated with the whole Flower Power, love and peace ethos. Chrissie and I spent all our free time with the hippies; we had barbecues, bonfires, parties, drinks, drugs, love-ins, everything you can think of at the beach that summer. I soon graduated from my safe nondescript wardrobe to more colourful, floaty clothes. The only black thing I owned after that was a floppy felt hat. I used to fix little bells on my belts or bags, or on a thong round my neck. I loved the sound of bells (still do).

In my own way I was dealing with the horrendous aftershock of the first hours of married life: the realization of the dreadful mistake I had made, and the almost unbelievable fact that no one on this earth had the slightest inkling of what I had gone through. At the time I was living purely in the moment, almost like a free spirit. In the back of my mind I knew it couldn't last, but for now I was going to make the most of every minute.

I found myself drawn towards a guy called Kaz. He was about eighteen, with long dark wavy hair, eyes the colour of hot chocolate and white, even teeth. When I touched him his skin was warm and smooth like velvet, and he moved in a way that was loose and graceful. He made his living by drawing portraits in charcoal, capturing holidaymakers down by the seafront. He's probably a surveyor now or an architect, but like the rest of us then he was just drifting, having a good time, experimenting with drugs, getting pissed, screwing around. We had a relationship for a while, and it was good. With no expectations, no jealousy, no angst, just a coming together and sharing of the good things. We made each other laugh, put the world to rights, smoked dope, cuddled and made love.

Although 'love and peace' was almost a national phenomenon throughout the Sixties this new culture had not yet influenced the older residents of this small town. They still clung to their pre-Sixties values. 'Fornication' was still a cardinal sin and was not to be condoned. Making love, however beautiful, was not for enjoyment, or for anybody but married couples.

Our presence as hippies in the town, although colourful and youthful, did slightly antagonize the locals. Occasionally it became like a game of chess with the two generations trying to outwit each other. This to us just became another element of fun and excitement.

Kaz's summer home was in a Bed and Breakfast, one of the establishments that reluctantly accepted the New Age hippy guests. He lodged there with two other friends, Rabbit and Jesus. The landlady was always referred to as 'Ma Bates'. She was a really scary woman and her tall, overweight, shapeless physique, large hands and feet made her look like a man in drag. I think her hair was dark although it was almost impossible to tell, as she always appeared in rollers. Her main attire seemed to be a flower-printed cotton wrap-around apron. At our occasional meetings, she frightened me with her disapproving stance: foot tapping, arms tightly folded, face that could be compared to a well-slapped arse!

Although situated in a nice area of the town, Ma Bates's Bed and Breakfast was the most run-down, dirtiest, smelliest doss house in the whole area. From the outside it looked very much the same as any of the others until you saw the windows, which never seemed to have been cleaned. Also, unlike the other Bed and Breakfasts, the guests were made up of young males who were possibly on the dole and probably doing drugs of some description. There seemed to be only one house rule, which was definitely no women. As you can imagine this rule became a bit of a challenge to Kaz and the other five in residence. Eventually this spirit of competition was passed on to whichever of us young ladies were in favour at the time.

Quite a bit of time and effort went into trying to outwit Ma Bates, and she was a formidable enemy, every bit as determined to keep us from her boys as we girls were to be with them. I don't think it was a religious thing, but I can't be sure as I never had the chance to hang around and find out. Her dialogue to me when she caught me was very Irish and direct. Amid the loud giggles of the other guests, some of the distinguishable words were 'hussy, fucking, brazen, out, off, five shillings'. This small vocabulary constituted most of her dialogue but it was never quite apparent in which order the words would appear.

Spending the night in Kaz's room at Ma Bates's could have been nominated as an SAS training course. The first obstacle was to get through the front door, across the hall and up the stairs without being seen. One useful tactic was to time your access to coincide with something very interesting on the television. Or we would create some form of distraction. Obviously Ma Bates had many years' experience and was battle-hardened and knew every tactic there was to prevent her one rule being broken. If caught in the room, there were two options: you could either pay the five shillings room rent or be thrown out anytime during the night.

Having jumped the first hurdle and reached the room, there was then the possibility of being caught on her nightly patrols. The times of these patrols followed no pattern that we could discern appearing to be quite random and indiscriminate. She would bang on the door and demand entrance. Our reactions to these intrusions were quite strange: we were all partly terrified by being caught and partly wetting ourselves laughing, depending on whether or not we had enough money to pay the rent. The boys would often hide us in the wardrobe but they had little in the way of clothing to use as camouflage. Crouched up naked with the vacant hangers, I soon discovered that nothing rattles more than an empty wardrobe. This was a ridiculous place to hide, but on the other hand it was hilariously funny. Other hiding places were behind the door, lying as flat as a pancake in the bed or in the dirt and dust under the bed. But alas, Ma Bates's long experience had given her a good knowledge of where to look, and had you not got the rent money you were out on your ear whether it was 3 a.m. or 6 a.m. She had no qualms about throwing young girls out onto the street at any hour of the morning.

However, Ma Bates was protective about her boys, and didn't blame them if they were caught with girls. To her we were just loose women, and the boys knew no better and couldn't be expected to control themselves.

Having had the Ma Bates experience, and not wishing to repeat the long walk back home in the early hours, nor the middle-of-the-night humiliating tongue-lashing, I became brave enough to take Kaz back to my humble quarters where we wouldn't have the excitement of running the gauntlet.

Still only teenagers, there was a great excitement and energy plus a sense of mischief in exploring our love making – feelings enhanced by the effects of smoking pot. On my part, there was also an underlying, desperate desire to enjoy and experience life to the full. Never escaping me for long, I knew that the day would come when I would be caged again.

My room, however basic, had become a welcoming haven where I could be myself. The strong cocktail of inhibited sexual desire, passion and affectionate together-ness with Kaz made the outside world disappear, only returning when I had to get up and put on my waitress' uniform.

These nights with Kaz became more frequent and the fear of being caught disappeared into insignificance. Often we would get up in the morning, shower together, embrace and I would then dress and make my way to the kitchen to start my breakfast shift.

One particular day, just before lunch, I walked into the kitchen and the assistant cook gave me a most strange look. She was skinny with blonde, frizzy hair and a long thin nose which she had the habit of looking down whenever she got into conversation with the junior staff. As I got near to her she started the strangest monologue about some of the interesting and often disgusting things that you could see from the top of a double-decker bus. She then went on to say how little Miss or Mrs Inno-cence, who appeared as though butter would not melt in her mouth, was actually something quite different. The monologue became stranger still when she started on about marriage vows, which had to be taken seriously. I was left completely confused, so I confronted her and asked her if she was trying to tell me something.

With her voice taking on a slightly higher tone, she seemed to get more excited. 'There's a bus stop outside your bedroom window, you know, and I come to work on a bus, it's a double-decker. I always sit on the top deck. You probably thought that because your window was small and high, nobody could see in, and that's where you're wrong young madam! I could see everything! I've never seen a man do that to a woman before, both completely naked. You should be ashamed of yourself; you're a married woman! Your husband is in the Forces; he's abroad for heaven's sake. Have you no shame?'

I was absolutely mortified, could feel the blood rushing up towards my head, but I tried my best to disguise how awful I felt. My defence mechanism clicked in with nuclear speed.

'I don't suppose it occurred to you to stop watching as soon as you realized you were spying on a very intimate, loving moment in someone else's life, did it?' And then in for the kill, 'Or is your life so sad that that's how you get all your cheap thrills?'

Deep down I just wanted the floor to open up and

swallow me – how many other people had been having a cheap thrill at my expense? At the same time, I couldn't help noticing her face. It truly was a picture, especially when I retaliated.

After a while the initial shock and embarrassment started to wear off and I began to see the funny side of it. All of us, including Kaz, had a good laugh about how we had shocked her. Amid the pot-enhanced giggles and laughter we started to imitate Ma Bates's strong Irish accent. 'Hussey, fucking, brazen, out, off, five shillings.'

But somewhere amid the fun and the haze that evening, I think I quietly asked myself: 'Is it time to move on?'

Chapter Eleven

STILL RUNNING PARALLEL, OF course, was my other life. I occasionally went home to see my parents and family, and Neil's family. I wrote letters to Neil full of empty news about work, and nothing much else. I suppose I ought to have felt guilty but I didn't. He was due back within a few weeks when a letter arrived saying he was being delayed by another couple of months. The relief was enormous but it was also made me more aware of the reality of his imminent return. I got to thinking, maybe I should just disappear. I wasn't at home anyway and he wasn't going to be back for another two months. Maybe he would never find me – perhaps he wouldn't even bother to look! I could be anywhere in two months.

Who was I kidding? Of course he would try to find me. No, he would definitely find me. Then what? Well, I suppose I could always pray for a quick death! So what then? Wait around for his return and walk into the cage/

prison of married quarters, handing him the key as I went through the door?

I'd told Chrissie a bit about Neil hitting me but nothing about the other abuse. I am a good keeper of secrets and I felt ashamed of how Neil treated me and blamed myself for his behaviour. Chrissie had arranged to go home for a short holiday, and on the day she was leaving I pulled her aside to talk to her. In a few moments of panic I had decided to run away and wanted to know if she would help me. Of course she said she would and I arranged to leave the hotel secretly and go with her that night. Unfortunately for me, Catherine overheard us making arrangements and insisted she came too, or she would tell Mr Jones. Chrissie didn't want to put her own job in jeopardy or her parents' friendship with the Jones's and I didn't want Mr Jones to know I was leaving him in the lurch, especially as I was on breakfast duty with Catherine at seven o'clock the next morning.

There was nothing else for it; I had to take little Miss Clumsy with me. As we made our plans, we realized that all of us leaving together could be a serious mistake. If Neil did arrive home earlier and came looking for me, it would be obvious I'd gone with Chrissie and she could get hurt. So she left in the afternoon and hitch-hiked home. Catherine and I worked our evening shift, packed our bags, sneaked out and caught the late bus. We travelled through the night and the stress, excitement and lack of sleep had worn us out by the time we got to Chrissie's parents' house. Our plan was to spend one night there, and then we would disappear.

When we arrived at Chrissie's home, her dad and sister weren't there but her mum was. Just as Chrissie had described her to me, she was indeed wonderful and 'cool'. She provided a delicious meal, comfortable beds for the night, tender loving care and all with no questions asked. The following day, armed with sleeping bags provided by Chrissie and with the bare essentials of our wardrobe, we set off on our great adventure. Catherine started as she meant to go on by complaining that her feet were killing her before we had gone two hundred yards down the road.

The following six weeks were just like a haze and I cannot recall all that much about them. I know we went up as far as John O'Groats and down as far as Land's End and visited lots of places in-between. We hitch-hiked everywhere, slept rough in sleeping bags in parks, on benches, on strangers' floors or on beaches, and we never felt we were in danger. We always tried to stay with women if we could, or in flats where at least some of the blokes had girlfriends. In this respect, I wasn't totally stupid.

Towards the end of the six weeks, we eventually ran

out of money and had no food, so we begged on the street. Fortunately, kind people always gave us something, and so we didn't starve.

I don't know whether the world was a safer place then or if it just seemed to be. We met lots of great people and had a really 'swinging' time. By that I mean we must have tried every drug known to man at least once, smoked dope and drank a lot (well, a lot for me). This may sound a bit incongruous but we didn't sleep around because that wouldn't have been safe. Anyway, it's a bit difficult getting two people into a single sleeping bag.

Slowly, as my thoughts became clearer, I realized I had decided that death was preferable to life with Neil. I'm not sure if I had always known that I wanted to kill myself and had been in denial, or if the idea just came to me on this journey. Maybe it was something to do with the drugs I was taking. Wherever the realization came from, it felt like the only way out for me.

Even with these desperate thoughts, although I had given up responsibility for myself, the responsibility for Catherine was a problem. I was going to have to try and get her home, or leave her with somebody to take care of her. She was hopeless, quite unable to look after herself.

Having accepted that I was going to die, I felt an

overwhelming desire to speak — possibly for the last time — to my mother. Not to tell her anything, just to hear her voice. She would think I was calling her from work and would never know where I was. We were not on the phone at home of course; in those days, very few people were. So a conversation with Mum entailed two phone calls, the first to my father's place of work, to leave a message telling her when I would call the telephone box at the end of the road.

When I made the call to my mother I hit the wall.

It turned out that Neil's paternal grandfather was dying and was asking to see me. My mother, completely unaware of the events of the last six weeks, had tried to reach me by telephoning the hotel a couple of days earlier. She had got the full fury of Mr Jones who was absolutely livid. I had not only left him in the lurch but Catherine, as it turned out, was no more a bit slow than I am. In fact, Catherine was actually not quite sixteen and thus underage. She had written to her parents and told them she was having a bit of a jaunt, and even sent the occasional postcard. Her long-suffering parents were apparently used to this behaviour from her, but by now they were threatening to involve the police unless she returned home immediately. My mother, who was understandably frantic, told me that I could possibly be charged with kidnapping.

Oh bugger! I never questioned nor considered how old she was, I just assumed she was eighteen. No wonder we all thought she was a bit on the slow side. All those years of looking after my baby brothers immediately kicked in. I knew I couldn't send her back on her own – she was just a child.

After this call, it took us a couple of days to get back home, and although our parents were relieved to see their daughters they were not exactly pleased with us. All the way home I kept reminding Catherine not to mention anything about drugs to her parents, or anybody else for that matter. I just thanked God she hadn't had sex with anyone.

It took a few days for things to settle down at home. My lifestyle over the last eight months remained a secret within my family. Neither Neil nor his family had the slightest inclination how I had survived his absence.

I did go to see Neil's grandfather in hospital; he was in a bad way. Then I had two weeks to prepare myself for Neil's homecoming. I felt like I was on death row. My moods were very up and down; my nerves were stretched taut like piano wire and I was very depressed. Then, the day before Neil was due back, his grandfather died of pneumonia. This is not going to help the situation I remember thinking to myself. This is definitely going to make the situation much, much worse.

Chapter Twelve

I T WAS A COLD, CLAMMY, drizzly morning in late July that perfectly matched my mood, as I waited in trepidation for Neil's train to arrive at the small local station. I felt that the rest of Neil's family were secretly relieved to pass on to me the responsibility of breaking the sad news to him.

Neil had not even been told that his grandfather was gravely ill. His grandmother had made the decision to keep this news from him as she did not want him to be sad and worried when he was so far away from home. No one had expected his grandfather to die quite as quickly as he did, and I think his grandmother had believed that Neil would have plenty of time to say his goodbyes. He was especially close to his grandfather who was more of a surrogate father to him after his own dad had died. No one knew how he would react, so here I was like a lamb to the slaughter. At least that's how I felt.

I had spent the previous two weeks trying to convince myself that the feeling of being in a deep, dark cave with no way out and the bubbling, hysterical panic and fear that threatened to engulf me were really just normal under the circumstances. I hadn't seen Neil for about eight months, now that was bound to feel strange, wasn't it? I was about to leave my family and everything I'd known to live a completely different life in a totally new part of the country. I didn't even know where that was going to be yet. That was exciting though, wasn't it?

Obviously all of the trying to convince myself everything was okay hadn't totally worked. Otherwise I wouldn't be fighting with myself now about whether I needed to rush to the loo to evacuate my bowels, or be sick on the platform.

At last I heard the train approaching the station, albeit ten minutes late. I hadn't been able to prepare myself properly for this moment, this first meeting with Neil on his return home, because I hadn't intended to be here. It was only the guilt I would have felt if I'd left him when his grandfather was dying that had stopped me sticking to my plan. I took deep breaths as I fought to gain control of my emotions and myself.

Neil appeared at the end of the platform and looked around. I was standing behind a pillar and he didn't see me, although I could see him. Just for a few seconds, before he bent down to pick up his cases, the look on his face was that of a disappointed and vulnerable child, a little boy lost. My heart went out to him and I hurried along the platform to greet him, all concerns for myself momentarily forgotten. We embraced and he seemed really pleased to see me. I asked him to sit on one of the benches on the platform. He was puzzled but reluctantly sat down amongst the jungle of potted plants, pansies, geraniums and roses that brightened the station. Holding his hand I told him about his grandfather.

Neil was obviously very shocked. His face went white and he was very quiet, but he let me take him in my arms, give him a cuddle and reassure him that everything would be all right. After about ten minutes he said he would like to drop his cases off at my parents' house then go and visit his grandmother and see his grandfather's body to pay his last respects. He spent a long time talking to his grandmother while I chatted to his aunt, then he went to see the body at the local undertakers. When he came back he was distraught, crying; I'd never seen him display such emotion. After about a quarter of an hour I could sense him starting to panic, as though the feelings were just too much for him. He couldn't get away from his grandmother's fast enough. He literally ran away, barely even saying 'goodbye, see you at the funeral'.

On the way back from his grandmother's house we called to see his mother. A courtesy call, he said, to let her know he was back. It was a very strange visit. Although she hadn't seen him for eight months and his grandfather had just died, she never even gave him a hug. He stood there, obviously hurting, hopping about from one foot to the other, wanting/needing a hug, a kind word, something.

She said, 'You're back then?'

He replied, 'Yep. This is me.'

Then she asked him when the funeral was and they talked about the arrangements.

That night he got drunk and never came to bed at all. The following day he slept all day and all night.

By the time Neil got up on the third day of his leave he was back to his old self, or should I say his normal self. He appeared in the kitchen at about nine thirty in the morning and, after greeting my mother, made a pointed but jokey comment about his wife being out of bed and in the kitchen in her dressing gown. My mother (ironically completely unaware of how she had smacked the nail right on the head) snapped back that surely I should not have to ask permission to get up in the morning. Neil smoothed things over by explaining how much he had missed me and Mum then busied herself in making tea and toast. When he was out of her view Neil jerked his head, forcefully indicating I was to go upstairs. Somehow I made my legs move, putting one foot in front of the other as far as the bedroom.

My clothes were laid out on the bed. I felt as though I was in a time warp. Time stood still, I'm not sure how long for, then I took a quick shaky breath, my mind went into overdrive and I started rushing around. Quick, quick, I kept saying over and over to myself, get ready, get out of here, don't let him catch you in this room. Hurry up, hurry up!

Back downstairs he was still sitting at the table. 'You didn't need to rush darling, I haven't finished my toast yet. Look at you, you're all flushed. Sure you're okay?' He was grinning at me. I'm sure he knew exactly how I was feeling. He was playing with me.

After he finished his tea and toast, we went for a drive and a chat. Neil apologized for not being himself since he arrived back, explaining that his grandfather's death had been a terrible shock. He thanked me for being so supportive and admitted he wasn't looking forward to the funeral, wishing it was all over. He was being so nice that I had almost lulled myself into a false sense of security when he suddenly went on to remind me of the rules. He expressed his displeasure that since he came home on leave I had not been obeying his rules. This morning, he said, was a prime example, I hadn't even asked permission to get up. Well, he was a reasonable man and as we were staying at my parents' he would let it go this time, but from now on it was business as usual. He went on to remind me how much he loved me and how he was going to take care of me *always*! Luckily I was not required to respond as my throat by now felt paralysed with fear, as my world began to close in around me once again.

The monologue continued with Neil imparting information about where his next posting was and that we would be moving in about three weeks' time. There seemed to be a part of me that was separate from me, merely observing what was happening. This observer noted with interest that nine months ago I would have been delighted to discover I was going to be living at the other end of the country to my family. However, my prince had turned back into a frog and I was now absolutely horrified. What the hell was I going to do?

Neil's voice brought me back from my inner panic and turmoil. He was telling me that after the funeral we would spend about a week here, keep things sweet. Then we would pack up my belongings, plus the wedding presents, put everything into the car and drive to his next posting and our married quarters, which was a flat. There wasn't that much stuff and one trip would do it, he said.

All I had to do in the meantime was behave myself and when we were settled in our own place things would be different. I wasn't quite sure what he meant by that, but I had a horrible feeling I wasn't going to like it.

He was incredibly sweet to me after that. Romantic, good fun, chatty – he was just great. I felt loved, even if I could never relax, never forget that I was living by his rules. We went out with friends and visited relatives. He charmed my mother and my grandmother, and got on well with my dad. On the day of the funeral he was very quiet and subdued, didn't show any emotion what-soever. I tried to get him to talk but he didn't want to. He just wanted it over with and forgotten, that's what he said. Apart from that one day, though, he was charm personified.

About a week later we packed up my stuff and the wedding presents, just as Neil had said we would. Then we drove all day to our new home and our new life together.

Chapter Thirteen

I DON'T REMEMBER HOW NEIL got hold of the key to our flat, and on that day the name of the road and the number of the flat did not stick in my mind. I was numb with fear. I did notice that we were on a large estate, with row upon row of houses and flats, probably looking like any other armed forces camp. The grey pebble-dashed flats were in blocks of four: two upstairs accessed by concrete steps at each end, and the two downstairs had a small open-plan lawn. Stone paths led to the blue front doors.

Daylight was just beginning to fade as Neil switched the car engine off. He said something about thinking we were never going to get here. I couldn't really take in what he was saying; I was too tired and too scared. He disappeared into the flat for a few minutes, I think to put the lights on. I stayed in the car; I hadn't been given permission to move yet. I was very aware that, because I was tired, I could make some trivial mistake that would result in me being hurt.

'Come on, sweetheart, let's go inside, you look absolutely shattered.'

Aah – I nearly jumped out of my skin – where the hell had he come from? He was always creeping around, and seemed like he was everywhere at once. I never even saw him come out of the front door.

With great reluctance I left the security of the car. My head was swimming and I couldn't catch my breath. I felt much like a sailor who's been at sea for a long time and takes his first steps on dry land again. I stumbled.

'Whoops, careful darling,' he said in a voice full of concern.

I managed to make it up the path. He was standing inside the door, holding it open for me. As I walked through, he said in a silky voice, 'Welcome to your new home.' Then he closed the door quietly behind me.

I felt and heard the door to my prison closing and locking as I fought to control my conflicting emotions. After all, Neil was being really sweet, so why was I being so dramatic? I just needed to get hold of myself, give myself a good talking-to, and sort myself out.

Look, this was dangerous behaviour; Neil was talking and I wasn't listening. That was one of the rules wasn't it, listen and do everything you are told? He was saying something about me looking around while he emptied the car. That it was late, so we'd just make up the bed tonight. Okay, so I will have a look around, right?

Well, I was standing in the hall; it was not very long and the walls were a cream-coloured emulsion. There was a table with a lamp on it, and the floor was covered in a black shiny paint. On the right, at the end of the hall, were two doors, one leading to the lounge, the other to the kitchen. On the left were two more doors to the bedrooms, and facing me at the end of the hall was the bathroom door.

Moving through the flat, I saw that the cream walls were throughout, as well as the black shiny floors, apart from the green and white floor tiles in the bathroom and kitchen. The medium-sized lounge contained a television, a cottage suite in a grey and white speckled material, and a long low coffee table. There was a small rug on the floor in front of the wall-mounted gas fire, and a couple of very naff prints on the walls.

One bedroom had a double bed with two bedside tables, and a chest of drawers, the style of which would best be described as utility. There was a wall closet to hang clothes in. The second bedroom was similar, except that it contained two single beds.

The bathroom was basic, a white suite with bathroom cabinet, but the kitchen was something else. It wasn't massive. It had a table and four chairs, gas oven, sink, etc. – all the normal basic requirements of that time, including a walk-in pantry – but, joy of joys, there was a washing machine and a refrigerator, neither of which we had at home. If only things had been different, I could have really been happy there.

Neil came into the kitchen with the last box, which he stacked neatly on the floor. As I looked around I realized that in his usual quiet and efficient way all the correctly labelled boxes and cases were now in the appropriate rooms just ready to be unpacked, arranged into apple pie order for the following day. He then plugged the television set in and invited me to stretch out on the sofa, informing me he was going to search out a fish and chip shop for some food and bottles of pop. He told me not to bother unearthing cutlery and crockery, as I was far too tired for that. 'Anyway,' he said, 'fingers were invented long before knives and forks.' He had put the water heater on saying that a bath would be nice, because travelling always made him feel grubby, and he was sure I probably felt the same.

I spent the time he was away trying to work out what would happen next. I wanted to get inside his head, but I was beginning to realize that the longer I knew him, the more I didn't know him at all. I was perplexed. A fight was going on in my head between the reality of what was actually happening at the moment, which seemed to be a nice scene – a normal young couple moving into their first home together – and my gut feeling and past experiences which told me something bad was going to happen. I didn't know what to do. I felt really frightened, but on the surface my fears appeared to be baseless.

When he came back we ate our supper, or more correctly he did, as I tried to swallow food around the lump in my throat. I felt as though I was choking and my nerves were totally on edge. He reached out to take my plate from me and I flinched.

He looked at me in that kind of amused way he had that never really reached his eyes, and he said he would run my bath.

Ten minutes later Neil called me into the bathroom, by which time I was shaking so much I couldn't undress myself. He just undressed me as though the fact that I was terrified was quite normal. He lifted me up, put me in the bath and proceeded to wash me. All the time he was talking to me in a quiet soothing voice, but what he was saying was not soothing at all. He was telling me that it was natural to feel scared, that it was okay. He understood, and I had got a lot to learn, and he had every confidence in me.

'I know that you love me and I love you, so we can

do this together. You want to make me happy, and you promised to love, honour and obey, and that's exactly what you are going to do. If you don't you will die, slowly and painfully. It's not going to come to that though, darling. So you don't need to worry on that score. Okay?'

On and on he went, all the time washing me, kissing me, stroking me. I didn't speak, I couldn't. But I wasn't expected to participate in the conversation, just to listen.

Then he got in the bath and told me to wash him – accompanied by more of the same monologue. Was he mad? Was I mad? What the hell was I doing here? How could I escape?

After our bath he made me perform oral sex on him. When he ejaculated into my mouth I turned away from him and tried to spit his sperm down the toilet. He grabbed me by the hair, and held my mouth closed and ordered me to swallow it. Afterwards I asked him if I could clean my teeth or rinse my mouth out, and he refused to let me do this. He said a tart like me should feel honoured to receive his sperm. I started crying and he just coldly informed me that crocodile tears would not work with him. After all I was his wife wasn't I? He had paid his seven shillings and sixpence marriage licence fee – he could use me anyway he wanted.

'If you need a pee, get a move on, I'm tired,' he drawled as he exited the bathroom.

When I entered the bedroom he was just finishing making up the bed. He had his back to me and continued chatting. 'You don't need to wear nightdresses anymore, I don't like them. I need to have instant access to all parts of you at any time.'

This cannot be happening to me; I must be in a nightmare that I am going to wake up from. I think I am going to be sick. What's he saying now? What's that something about a sleeping bag? I – I don't understand. What's happening?

Neil was saying something about how we must start as we mean to go on, and I must learn to know my place. Trying to spit out his sperm was a very bad thing for me to do, and I must be punished. He was trying to train me to be a good and obedient wife, but it's like training a puppy. So, tonight I would be in the dog-house. He put a sleeping bag on the floor on his side of the bed, and told me to sleep there. 'Don't leave your bed without permission,' he warned me as he turned out the light.

I tried to sob quietly, but it's very hard when you feel as though your heart is breaking. I was alone and vulner-able, a long way from home and with no one to turn to, and no money. I should have just killed myself before Neil got home. I wished I had!

'Stop that noise, or you'll get something to cry about,' said Neil in a cold quiet voice.

I know I must have fallen asleep eventually, the sleep of the mentally, emotionally and physically exhausted. I know this because I was dimly aware of an uneasy blackness, punctuated by monsters, fire and wild animals snarling and chasing me, trying to devour me. I was running around and around in ever-decreasing circles then catapulted back into full consciousness as a dragon breathing fire was about to consume me. Sweating, shaking and gasping for breath I was conscious of a brief feeling of relief as I realized I must have been having a nightmare. Then the reality of my situation clicked back in. My real life was much worse than any nightmare I could possibly imagine.

If Neil had been aware of my hippy lifestyle when he was overseas he would perhaps have recognized the irony of making me sleep on the floor. I had slept in much worse places over the past few months; at least it was warm and dry, if a trifle hard. In fact it was infinitely preferable to sharing a bed with him.

I couldn't locate myself within the room for the hammering noise inside my head, like cogs in a wheel chasing each other round and round as I searched for some means to escape. My ears couldn't distinguish between sounds coming from inside my head and inside or outside of the room. Everything was muffled by a booming sensation that matched the frantic beating of my heart as I fought down the vomit that kept rising into my throat. At the same time, my bowel was having an argument with my bladder as to which would evacuate itself first, providing of course that the muscles in my legs, stiff and paralysed with fear, would carry me as far as the bathroom.

I kept telling myself to 'ssh, ssh,' keep calm, be quiet, everything will be okay, don't worry, just be calm. First things first, first you need the loo. I just had to keep talking, calming myself down. Eventually I realized it was very quiet in the room. It was a bit dark because the curtains were closed and I didn't know what time it was. I couldn't see if Neil was still in bed, I couldn't hear him breathing, and the bedroom door was shut. I really need to go to the toilet, I thought; I don't know how long I can hang on. Is he there? Shall I risk having a look? What if he's still in bed and he sees me. What will he do? I couldn't hear any noise outside the bedroom either, so he must still be asleep. I can't hear him breathing though. Surely I should be able to hear something, shouldn't I? I'll wait a while – no, I can't, I'm desperate for the loo.

Very slowly I raised myself up and peeped over the side of the bed. Immediately my eyes locked into those blue, cold eyes.

'Feeling brave this morning are we?' He propped himself up on one elbow and smiled.

'Neil, I'm desperate for the toilet. Please can I go to the toilet? I've been trying to wait until you wakened up but I'm sorry I can't wait any longer.' I felt sick to my stomach when I heard my pleading, apologetic, whiny voice. Part of me wanted to jump on the bed and stab him.

He told me to put the kettle on after I'd been to the bathroom and, guess what, I felt grateful. I don't know who I despised most at that moment, him for what he was doing to me, or myself for getting into this situation and now being pathetically grateful for even the smallest acts of kindness. As it happened he'd already been out for milk, bread, butter, tea, coffee and other basics. He had also unpacked every box and suitcase. The flat was immaculate, a place for everything and everything in its place – his words not mine.

I asked for my clothes but he said no, not yet, maybe after breakfast. He said he had always wanted to watch me cooking bacon and eggs for him naked, the sick bastard. Panicking I pulled myself up short, not quite sure if I had spoken my thoughts aloud. He was looking at me a bit weirdly, but he was talking about helping by setting the table. Then he said, 'Don't bother making any for yourself, you can have fruit. I've noticed you must have put about half a stone on while I was away. Fat women turn me off. You're on a diet.'

The thought of having to sit at the table and eat with him made me want to vomit so that came as a bit of a relief anyway. Bananas are a lot easier to swallow than greasy bacon and egg, which he consumed with relish whilst I was secretly praying it would choke him. Unfortunately no such luck.

Afterwards I was allowed to dress and he supervised the shopping list. We went shopping together and on our return he taught me how he wanted the shopping put away. Shelves and tins had to be wiped, everything had a place and that place was where Neil wanted it to go, nowhere else. I had to make notes to ensure I didn't forget. He told me about food, what I was allowed to eat and in what quantities. I had to write that down too. Sometimes (not always) after Neil went back to work, he would leave out on the side the food for the day: what had to be cooked for the evening meal, what I was allowed to eat for lunch. Then if he thought I had been 'stealing' food he would lock the pantry.

The flat wasn't excessively large and it appeared I would have plenty of time to clean it. Neil informed me

I would not be allowed to get a job and he wished to start a family immediately. He flushed my prescription for contraceptive pills down the toilet. By the end of the first day in our new home, even I was beginning to accept that there would be no such thing as 'talking things over and making mutual decisions', not in our relationship.

Neil congratulated me on his delicious lunch, two rounds of ham salad sandwiches with cheese and onion crisps, apple pie and ice cream, and coffee. He ate this in the lounge stretched out on the sofa watching television. I, on the other hand, was allowed one slice of bread with salad filling and an apple. I had to eat sitting on the floor in the kitchen because Neil had noticed a spark of rebellion in my eyes when he told me what I was allowed for lunch. After all, he had said, I was allowed a cup of coffee and it was for my own good. I had then been subjected to one of his monologues of self-justification, along the lines of:

Had he made me put weight on in the first place? No he hadn't.

Did I think he wanted to be deprived of my company over lunch when he hadn't seen me for eight months? No he didn't.

He was only doing this because he loved me. All he asked was for some cooperation, some compromise from me.

Did he have to provide all the love as well as all the caring? Why did I have to make everything such hard work?

The thoughts churned in my head. Maybe it is me, am I just being childish, rebellious? Do I just want everything all my own way? You have to make compromises in any relationship. I'll try and make more of an effort. Try harder to do things Neil's way, see if that eases the situation. After all if he's happy then surely I will be too. Just because our relationship isn't how I thought it was going to be, doesn't mean it won't work. Neil's probably feeling really insecure or something. His grandfather has just died, he probably needs reassurance, and I shouldn't give up at the first hurdle.

After lunch we went for a long walk. 'Exercise is good for you,' Neil said. Well, I agreed with him but I was feeling really knackered and we walked for what seemed like miles.

'Helps keep your weight down, darling,' he smiled across at me as he sauntered along by my side.

I sighed, 'I know and I'm not complaining but will we be able to go home soon, because I am a bit tired now?'

He pulled me towards him, nuzzled my neck and then whispered in my ear, 'We'd better get back then. Don't want you being too tired to play later, do I? That would be terribly disappointing.'

My knees seemed to give way as my stomach did a nose dive. I think if he hadn't had his arm round me I would have collapsed.

'Better get a cab then, sweetheart. I hope that's passion you've been overcome by,' he laughed.

I looked up at him, right into those wintry blue eyes. I guess that was when I finally realized, the lights were on but there was nobody home.

Chapter Fourteen

I PASSED THROUGH THE FRONT door before Neil and headed quickly for the bathroom. He asked me where I was going because I hadn't asked permission. I apologized but explained I was so desperate for a 'wee' I had forgotten.

'Hurry up then, don't keep me waiting, I'm hungry.'

I sat on the toilet, fist clamped firmly in my mouth to stop the scream from escaping, tears running down my face, snot running from my nose. What could I do? What could I do? Neil knocked on the bathroom door. I shouted I was sorry I forgot to ask about going to the toilet.

'Look, it's not important, love,' he said. 'You know how much I love you. I just want to show you how much I love and care for you. Come on out now, it's okay.'

He didn't sound angry, but then he never did. I

couldn't sit in the bathroom forever and he seemed okay about everything. I blew my nose, washed my hands and face and slowly opened the door. I couldn't see him; maybe he was in the kitchen. He'd said he was hungry.

I turned left to walk into the kitchen; suddenly he came from behind, from the second bedroom. He grabbed me by the hair and before I could scream clamped his other hand over my mouth. He pulled me backwards into the bedroom; I was so shocked I started to struggle. He rabbit-punched me in the back. The pain was excruciating and I couldn't get my breath as he kicked my legs out from underneath me. His arm was tightly around my neck and as I was choking he was talking.

'Ssh, ssh, remember to be a silent screamer, practise being quiet and in control.' He repeated it over and over, calmly and quietly, like he was asking me if I wanted milk in my coffee or something. I was panicking like hell and all I could think over and over in my head was, 'He's a fucking nutter, he's a bloody maniac, he's going to fucking kill me!'

There was a chair in the bedroom, upright like a kitchen chair, and suddenly I saw he had handcuffs and, Jesus Christ, he was handcuffing me to the chair. Two pairs of handcuffs, one for each wrist. He tied my ankles to the chair legs with neckties. Then he started kissing me. His tongue was so far down my throat he was choking me and I couldn't move, couldn't escape from him and what he was doing to me.

'There now, that's better. Told you I was hungry, didn't I, love?'

'You said it was all right, you wanted to show me how much you loved me.'

He looked at me with total contempt; his eyes were like two hard grey flints. 'I lied about the first bit, but don't worry, I am going to show you how much I love you.'

He reached over and began to undo the buttons of my blouse, slowly. He said he wasn't sure whether he wanted me to cooperate while he undressed me because actually he quite fancied just ripping it off. He really liked the blouse though and it had cost him quite a bit. I could tell by his eyes he was weighing up these options and I tried to move away from him as he parted the front of my blouse and slipped it off my shoulders. At least now I knew why I had not been permitted the luxury of wearing a bra that morning. I was trying to twist my body away from his hands as his fingers reached for my nipples.

'Don't do that,' he said in a dangerously quiet voice. 'These are mine, to play with and do with whatever I want, whenever I want. Don't ever try to stop me enjoying what is mine. Or you will be sorry, very sorry indeed. Do you understand, bitch?'

My blood ran cold, the hairs on the back of my neck stood up as I nodded my head. With a determined look on his face Neil ripped the blouse from my body, twisted it round and round into a rope and slapped my breasts with it until the tears ran down my face. Silent tears of desperation and hopelessness.

'That's good,' he murmured in an encouraging voice, 'see you can do it. Nice and silent, obedient, that's a good girl.'

He was kissing me and licking my tears. I was sick with fear, my whole body shaking. He told me that was because I really wanted him to fuck me but I knew this wasn't true. He kept repeating it over and over: 'You really need it now. You really want me to fuck you, don't you? I'm not ready for you yet so you'll have to wait. You're a hot bitch. Can't get enough of it, can you? Can't get enough of me, can you?'

He had gone to the bathroom for baby oil and was rubbing it into my breasts, massaging my nipples, putting his hand down the front of my jeans, undoing the button, unzipping them. I was still tied and handcuffed. I couldn't move, I couldn't escape and the words kept going round and round in my head. 'Like a bitch on heat.' Neil

caressing me, touching, saying, 'You are so beautiful.'
Hot sizzling sensations began to shoot through my body.
Now he was soothing me where before he had hurt me,
confusing me . . . telling me I was feeling things I knew
I wasn't . . . then making me feel them, or making me
think I was feeling them. Eventually it didn't matter,
nothing mattered, and anything was better than being
hurt, wasn't it?

I was dimly aware that my legs were being untied
and handcuffs were being unlocked. He was behind me.
'Stand up sweetheart, I think it's time we relieved you of
these cumbersome jeans.'

I struggled to stand. I don't know how long I had
been on that chair, it seemed like forever. I tried to use
my hands to lever myself up, only to discover they were
now handcuffed behind me.

'Please Neil, you're really scaring me.' My voice was
like a croak because my throat and mouth were so dry
with fear.

'Good, that was my intention.' His voice was dangerously low. 'Fear's a good smell, it turns me on. Speaking
of being turned on, let's see how wet you are, shall we
darling?'

Yanking me off the chair he peeled my jeans down as
far as my knees. I was naked underneath. He told me that

blokes envied him because I was so beautiful and I belonged to him. Looking into my eyes he slipped his hand in-between my legs.

'Mmmm, nice to have your desire and passion confirmed,' he whispered in my ear as he leaned over and pulled me in closer.

I felt so vulnerable and ashamed. Like a slave being sold naked at an auction, being poked and prodded like a piece of meat. Neil picked me up and took me through to the lounge where my jeans were discarded. He told me to sit on the easy chair. Not easy when your hands are handcuffed behind you. Being the gentleman he was he explained to me that he wanted to 'finger-fuck' me. To facilitate this he would like me to sit with my bottom on the edge of the chair and my legs apart. To make it easier for me he then handcuffed my hands in front because he didn't want me to be too uncomfortable at this stage in our 'play'. He chatted away as though he was discussing how to hang curtains or make scrambled eggs. I concentrated very hard on trying not to feel anything – just surviving. Don't focus on the fear, concentrate on taking nice deep breaths. Breathe in through your nose and out through your mouth. I can do this, I will survive.

Breathing in to the count of five.

'Shuffle your bottom to the edge of the chair darling.'

Breathing out to the count of five.

'Good, now open your legs nice and wide . . . ummm lovely.'

Breathing in to the count of five.

'You are so wet, such a nice tight cunt, smell good too.'

Breathing out to the count of five.

'Do you like it when I rub your clitty darling? Talk to me.'

Breathing in to the count of five.

'Please, Neil, please just . . .' Breathing out to the count of five.

'Begging, yes, yes, I like that. Clever girl, very clever girl.'

Breathing in . . . out . . .

I don't know how long it went on for. How long it took my traitorous body and/or my weak, pathetic mind to betray me into orgasm. But betray me it did, or maybe it was just the only way I could survive. I don't know. I guess he would have just continued until orgasm so the sooner it happened, the sooner it would be over. After I climaxed he took off his trousers, sat in the chair and made me sit on top and have intercourse with him. I felt dirty, used, ashamed and then relieved when afterwards he removed the handcuffs. He promised that after I had cleaned up the mess in the bedroom I could have a bath before I ran one for him.

He walked into the bathroom looking all smug and sated just as I was running his bath. Neil told me I had made a good job of cleaning the bedroom then said he wanted a bath in peace and quiet. He told me to make a meal, giving me instructions on what we would both have to eat, and then he looked at me and started to laugh.

'You won't need that big bath towel wrapped around you. I've drawn the curtains in the kitchen, it is quite late anyway. Here, sweetheart, let's try this hand towel. You know I like those beautiful breasts exposed and that tiny waist will easily accommodate this towel. Look, see how it just won't quite reach at the front so I get to see your pubes too. God, I'm such a lucky guy. Come and give your husband a kiss before you go.'

I heard pounding in my head again and my breathing had gone weird. My breathing was really starting to worry me. I was hyperventilating a lot, feeling dizzy and nauseous. I was disorientated a lot of the time.

Like a robot I made food. He ate. I couldn't, but he said I must. Then he rabbited on about not taking too much to heart about what he'd said about my weight, it was only about half a stone. We would soon lose that, wouldn't we? The great thing about our relationship, he said, was that because we loved each other we could do anything. I forced food down in between sips of water and was dimly aware that as well as being a psycho, Neil was also an egomaniac.

While I was washing the dishes he came up behind me and started fondling my breasts. I went into a total panic. I was absolutely frantic on the inside and totally still and motionless on the outside. He told me to continue with what I was doing. I tried, I really did, but within about a minute I was retching from fear into the washing-up bowl.

'Don't worry darling, you'll soon get used to it.' His voice sounded quite sympathetic. 'Tell you what. Why don't I finish that? You go and tuck yourself into bed. You deserve a good night's sleep. You've done well today, I'm very pleased with you.'

My relief was overwhelming, and there it was again, that feeling of being grateful for any small kindness. My head felt battered and as I lay in bed all I could think was: this is now my life, this is it. How am I going to survive? Can I escape? What can I do? What would happen if or when I got pregnant? My petrified mind would not even let me go there. Sleep, when it came, was once again filled with monsters and wild animals, hellfire, whips and chains.

God please help me. No one else could or would.

Chapter Fifteen

IN MY NIGHTMARE I COULDN'T move. I was lying on my side on a bed with my hands and feet tied. Someone behind me was touching me, stroking me all over. I was blindfolded, there was a gag in my mouth – the only two senses left for me to experience the world through were hearing and smell. Someone was breathing erratically somewhere near my left ear, their breath was hot on my shoulder. The bedsprings creaked as 'the someone' shifted their position on the mattress. A faint smell of spicy aftershave as 'the hands' began to move me onto my back. My body was slick with the sweat of fear; panic had made the muscles of my body tense and rigid. As I was slowly turned onto my back, a long, silent scream became trapped behind the gag stuffed inside my mouth . . .

'Darling, wake up, wake up, it's only a dream. It's just a bad dream, wake up sweetheart. Come on darling,

I'm here, you're safe, sshh, sshh, everything's okay.' Neil was gently shaking my shoulder as my eyes flew open and I struggled up through the fog of sleep into full consciousness. Yet again there was the slowly dawning realization that 'awake and conscious' was fairly similar to 'asleep and unconscious'. The only difference at this stage in our relationship between my dream and reality was that Neil did not need to use a gag on me. After living with him on camp for a few weeks I was now quietly submissive. He only tied or handcuffed me because, in truth, it turned him on, not because he needed to. I had learned from experience that to defy him in any way only brought further punishment.

'Are you okay? You were moaning and groaning. Sounded like a really bad dream, bit of a nightmare was it?' He pulled me in close, kissed my hair as I fought down my instinct to struggle and push him away.

'Don't know really,' I lied. 'Can't remember, something about being chased, running away and falling down I think. Is it okay to go to the toilet please, Neil?'

'Soon. I need to use you first. Climb on here and give this some of your expert attention.' He pulled back the bedclothes to reveal his erection and my heart sank, I must have hesitated because he roughly grabbed my arm. 'Now,' he ordered. 'Let's see if you can get it right this time, shall we, save yourself a beating.' He put his hands on my hips, which he said he would use to help guide me. 'Look into my eyes,' he commanded, 'don't look away.' I had to try not to think about anything except getting this right, pleasing him.

If I start thinking about how much I hate him, how he makes my skin crawl, or how terrified I am about what he'll do if I don't please him, he will know. He'll see it in my eyes. He's so bloody clever he knows everything that I'm thinking and feeling before I even know it myself.

After it was over, to my relief, he said it wasn't bad for council house trash. I still had to wait my turn for the bathroom though.

After breakfast Neil decided that as the weather was sunny and warm we may as well tidy up the garden. My first thought was, yuk gardening, I hate it. My second was, well at least I get to wear clothes. I should have known better. Well, to be fair I did get to wear some clothes. However, a short-sleeved low-cut tee shirt, no bra, and a short skirt with the briefest of panties is not my ideal gardening attire. I did screw up my courage and tentatively suggest maybe jeans would be better for gardening. All I got in reply from Neil was a throwaway comment about 'better for whom?'

Neil mowed the lawn while I had to trim the edges with a pair of shears. It was not the easiest of tasks, clipping away in my skimpy gardening gear whilst attempting to retain my modesty. A few people stopped for a chat. The neighbours seemed friendly enough – the woman from the flat next door brought us each a cup of tea. She said her husband was stationed abroad but would be back sometime in January. She had children below school age and invited me round for coffee anytime. 'It would be nice to have some company, especially adult conversation for a change.' Her name was Janet and she seemed really nice and friendly. I liked her.

Just as we were finishing the lawn two friends of Neil's turned up. I was on my way round to the back of the flats to put the shears and the lawnmower in the garden shed but Neil called me back. I walked over and Neil took my hand and pulled me in front of him so that he was standing behind me, with his arm round my waist.

'Eat your heart out, lads, this is my beautiful wife. Isn't she gorgeous? Darling, these are two good mates of mine, Pete and Lenny. We've served together a long time, shared most things haven't we, even women at times. Not this one though, this one's strictly off limits lads and don't you forget it.'

They were laughing, kidding around like a bunch of pubescent schoolboys. All the time Neil's hands were all over me. And Pete and Lenny's eyes never left Neil's hands. Neither of them made eye contact with me, not once – they were too busy ogling my body. I was so embarrassed, I could feel myself starting to blush. I felt like a tart, a non-person. I just wanted the ground to open up and swallow me. All of a sudden came a spark of something I hadn't felt for a long time – a flash of anger. Like lightning it came zigzagging up from somewhere deep inside me where it had been buried, smothered with fear and self-loathing.

For a split second I forgot about danger, reprisal, control, obedience. I pushed Neil's hands away, muttering something about putting the lawnmower away and stomped off round the back and into the flat. I could still hear them laughing and chatting for about another five minutes while I crashed about the flat trying to calm down. I was aware that I was crying but not silent self-pitying whimpering. Loud, gasping, angry sobs of rage and frustration. I threw myself onto the bed, kicking my feet and flailing my fists like a child having a tantrum. Thoughts and words – I hate you, you bastard, I have to escape, I have to get away – going round and round inside my head. Thumping the pillows, anger like a white-hot heat inside me, filling up all of my body. How could he? How dare he treat me like that, and in front of his friends?

He treated me like some kind of whore, something he owned. I felt vulnerable and exposed. He made me feel that all his friends saw when they looked at me was a sex toy. Nice bum, oh and by the way, great tits. Every man's sexual fantasy, always up for it, yeah that was me. Well no more; enough was enough. I was punching the wall now. Yes, that felt good, hurting yourself on the outside takes the pain away from inside.

He came quickly from behind, practically riving my hair out by the roots as he pulled me backwards away from the wall and off the bed.

'I'd much prefer it if you left the chastisement to me, you ungrateful little bitch. After all the time, effort and love I've put into you and this relationship you show me up like that in front of two of my oldest friends. Then I come in here and look at you, totally out of control. Sometimes I wonder if you're mentally ill. It would explain a lot about you and your behaviour.'

He was holding me by my hair, pulling it so tight the skin on my face felt as though it was being stretched. My eyes were watering, my head throbbing, as fear overwhelmed the anger of seconds before. 'Quite amusing, your little tantrum,' he laughed as he held up something for me to see that I didn't at first recognize. It looked a bit like a belt but it was too small. 'Like all masters and their puppies, I guess it's a long, slow process.' I was totally mesmerized, numb with shock as he fastened what I now recognized as a dog's collar round my neck. Neil made a big show of adjusting it so that it wasn't too tight, he didn't want it to choke me — how caring was that!

'Pull down your panties and lift up your skirt for me, darling, it's time for your punishment. Bend over the bed, there's a good girl.' On some level I was conscious that he was unbuckling the belt of his jeans but I was feeling really weird, like I wasn't in my body any more. I couldn't bear to be here, it was too much. How much longer, how much more? As though in a dream I did what he told me. As I bent over the bed he told me to open my legs slightly. I just did it; he lightly caressed me in-between my legs as I watched from somewhere above myself, detached somehow, feeling but not feeling. Then, he beat me across my bottom and thighs. I have no sense of how many times he hit me or how long it went on for. It hurt, but it didn't really hurt because I was only watching myself being beaten. Afterwards, he pulled up my panties, made me say thank you and apologize for my behaviour.

I felt nothing, yet somewhere inside me I knew it was impossible to feel nothing. I wasn't sure where exactly — maybe inside my head — was a knob, like a heat setting for an oven, that was labelled feelings. My oven setting had been full but now it was set on low.

Then Neil made coffee, which was served up with his usual monologue of homespun philosophy about love, marriage, relationships, particularly ours. I wasn't required to participate in this diatribe, just appear to be listening. He made me sit which was uncomfortable, my bottom and thighs were hot and hurt like hell. They were really stinging and I was relieved when Neil decided to veer off on one of his apparent tangents and suggested that after gardening a bath was a good idea.

'We just need to burn this rubbish in the garden first. Not much point in having a bath 'till after that, is there?' He asked it like a question, but I didn't get the feeling he required me to answer. In fact I started to feel a bit nervous and wonder what was coming next. I didn't have to wait long. He had disappeared into the spare bedroom and came back with a cardboard box full of what he obviously wanted to burn. On top of the box was my black felt, hippy hat. I had kept it for sentimental reasons, and it had been in the front pocket of my suitcase with one of my small bells. He put the box down on the kitchen table and picked up the hat, remarking that he had never seen it before. I thought, 'shit'.

'One of the waitresses at the hotel gave it to me as a leaving present. Nice of her wasn't it? I just kept it because she loved that hat and it wouldn't have been nice to throw it away after she gave it to me.'

'And this?' he said, holding up the bell between his thumb and index finger.

'James and Joseph bought me that for my birthday. You know how much I really love the sound of bells.' The adrenalin surge of fear had lent a sharpness to my brain, enabling me to instantly think up a believable lie. I could feel the sweat pouring out of me, I am sure I was blushing and I could not gauge from Neil's cold, measured stare whether he really believed me or was saving up some terrible retribution for me later.

Neil had never asked me about my social life during the time he was abroad. He only ever asked about my job and the people at work. I don't think it ever occurred to him that I would have dreamed of having a life outside of work. I think he believed he had already gained control over me through violence and fear before he left the UK and that it would never have entered my head to deviate from what he would have considered appropriate behaviour. Consequently he knew nothing about my hippy lifestyle, or my walkabout, and I didn't intend he should ever find out.

From his jeans pocket he took out a short length of red ribbon. 'See this,' he said, 'this is tarts' ribbon, for whores. Come here.' He threaded it through the hoop in the top of the bell, as I stood quaking before him, and attached it to the ring on the dog collar around my neck. 'Now, just like my very own little puppy I'll always know exactly where you are, won't I? Not too tight is it, your little collar?' His finger gently traced a line along my cheekbone, down to my chin; he kissed me, a long deep kiss that left me feeling beaten.

'Right, let's burn the rubbish. Bring your hat, darling,' he said briskly. I trailed after him into the garden. He soon had a fire going. I was sick with sadness for my wild summer as he ordered me to throw my one symbol of freedom and my happy memories onto the fire. As I followed him back into the flat I felt totally drained and exhausted. He, on the other hand, was buzzing, charismatic, powerful – making me feel hopeless and powerless obviously turned him on.

We had a bath together; I think I was in shock as I felt sleepy and not with it. Like a zombie I just obeyed orders, so we had sex in the bath. Afterwards he said he would cook. I couldn't have cared less, I was too exhausted to eat but I wasn't hungry anyway.

'What should I do with my new little pet?' he said, putting his finger in his mouth and pretending to look thoughtful. He was really enjoying his new, sick little game I thought to myself. He left the bathroom and reappeared a couple of minutes later with the sleeping bag and something else I couldn't quite see. 'We forgot to put your nice new collar on after your bath, darling. Here we go. Not uncomfortable is it? Now, we'll just clip this lead on and put your doggie bed down in the kitchen and you can watch Daddy while he cooks. Come on then, good little bitch.'

My brain could no longer comprehend what was happening to me as he led me into the kitchen, plonked the sleeping bag on the floor by the table, ordered me to sit, and stuck the end of the lead under the table leg forcing me to lie down. He was treating me like an animal, and that's how I felt, like a cornered, trapped animal. What would he do next? Had he totally flipped? He kept walking past and stroking me, my hair, my body, patting me, calling me good girl. I felt like my brain was in meltdown; I had to shut it all down. I think I fell asleep after a while but I don't know if it was for a few seconds, minutes, half an hour, I have no idea. When I woke up he was finishing eating his food. He told me I didn't get to eat today because of my atrocious behaviour.

'Let's take your bed into the lounge.' He released the lead from under the table leg and ordered me to bring the sleeping bag, then he led me into the other room. 'Now, can you be trusted to sit quietly in your bed and stay off the furniture or do I have to put your lead under the chair leg?' his stern voice enquired. Not used to playing the game, not knowing the rules, I just stood there, my eyes darting about the room, looking for a means of escape, not daring to make eye contact.

'Well?' said the stern voice. I was feeling sick and in

desperate need of a wee. And to make matters worse I was now in such a panic I couldn't remember the question. Oh bugger, what was the question? Something about . . . something about . . . think, think . . . furniture, staying off the furniture . . . that was it.

'Yes,' I whispered.

'Yes what?' He was starting to sound testy now but what was the right answer? I didn't know because I couldn't remember what the question was.

My mouth and throat went dry and my tongue felt too big for my mouth. I was breathing too fast, perspiring, really needed to pee. Oh God! What was the correct answer? Casually, he lit a cigarette and I could feel my eyes getting wider and wilder with fear and panic. He jerked me towards him by the dog lead; I felt the pull around my throat and a momentary pain in my neck. Taking a long drag from the cigarette Neil looked at me coolly, then held it close to my nipple but not quite touching. I could feel the heat from its tip, but it did nothing to help me remember the question therefore I still couldn't think of the right answer.

'Please Neil, I need to go to the bathroom, please can I go now, please?'

He looked at me with total disappointment and such a sympathetic look on his face. 'Darling, that was the wrong answer, poor you.' Quickly and in a very controlled way he touched the lighted end of the cigarette to my nipple three times, dab, dab, dab. I was hardly aware he had done it until it was over.

'Hurry up, you've got one minute, I'm timing you. Then I want you here, on your doggy bed on the floor by my chair while I watch television, where all good bitches should be, by their master's side, quietly, obediently.'

If I'd had any fight left in me that day I would probably have considered cutting my wrists with a razor blade or a knife, but one minute wasn't very long. I was too scared, too ground down, hurting too much, too shocked, whatever. I went to the loo and then sat on my bed beside him and endured. I was totally helpless and at his mercy. I slept on the floor in the bedroom that night on my 'doggy bed'. Physically I hurt all over but emotionally the pain was much, much worse. I was without hope, desperate, with no one to turn to.

Chapter Sixteen

M Y WORLD WAS SOON reduced down to what felt like an extremely narrow, dark tunnel. Neil was in control of every area of my life, financial, emotional, physical, mental, social. I felt suffocated, frightened and very much alone.

Like a hostage in a foreign prison I was isolated and totally at the mercy of my jailer, not knowing what each day would bring, but always afraid of what it might. Neil had virtually cut off any direct contact with my family and friends. He always read and censored my letters, both written and received. We had no private telephone and I was not allowed to leave the house without him. He took me for a walk either before or after work and we shopped together at the weekends for groceries. He continued to chose and buy all my clothes, shoes, make-up and jewellery and told me when and how to wear them. He even came to the hairdressers with me and very charmingly gave instructions on how he wanted my hair done.

When Janet from next door offered her neighbourly friendship, this one small lifeline was immediately blocked. Neil told me I was not to have any contact with her at all, unless he was present. He, on the other hand, was always popping next door for coffee and a friendly chat, and to play with her children. Once again, the little candle in the darkness of my miserable existence, my one chink of light, had been snatched away from me.

Neil had been detailed to go on a forty-eight hour exercise, but only broke the news to me on the morning he was due to leave. I was washing up his breakfast dishes (I had not been allowed to have any breakfast myself) but my head was in a whirl; here was my chance to escape. I could feel hope begin to flap its wings inside my breast. Neil was banging around in the bedroom and I presumed he was quickly getting his kit together for the exercise, but soon realized he was making far too much noise for that. Suddenly my intuition made me feel distinctly uneasy and uncomfortable. I was wishing he would just go, and leave me free from this pretence. Every day it was becoming more and more difficult to act normally and disguise my eagerness to escape.

'Time for you to use the bathroom darling. I'll have to be going soon.' I was so wrapped up in my own thoughts, I nearly jumped out of my skin on discovering he was actually in the kitchen with me. He was always sneaking about. Without question, I automatically headed towards the bathroom, thinking he may demand sex yet again before he left the house. I planned to spend as much time in the bathroom as possible, hoping that I could avoid what, depending on his mood, could be further sexual abuse, and praying that there would be no time before he had to leave.

As I was washing my hands Neil came strolling into the bathroom. He leaned against the wall next to the sink, and as he crossed one foot over the other, I felt panic slowly rising within me. My stomach began to tighten and my breathing became faster. He said, 'Time's running out and I need to prepare you before I go.' My ears began to pound, I felt sick, sweaty. He took hold of my arm to guide me from the bathroom, down the hall, into the bedroom.

It took me a couple of minutes to orientate myself. Although it was daylight outside, the curtains were drawn and there was a blanket over the curtain rail. No light appeared to be coming through the window at all. Out of the bedroom he had created a black cell! He had removed the ornaments, pictures, make-up and small pieces of furniture from the room – only leaving the dressing table in the far corner (but not the little stool I usually sat on when applying my make-up). Next to the bed was a potty like the big one my nana had at home.

Neil made his way over to the walk-in wardrobe, turned the key in the lock and put it in his pocket. Taking my hand he led me towards the bed.

'What? What's hap—'

'You didn't really think I was going to leave you here all on your own with no guidance from me, did you?'

'I'll be okay, I promise.'

'You will be now,' said Neil, as he pushed me onto the bed and grabbed hold of my left wrist. 'Of course it won't be first-class accommodation, but I've joined these four pairs of handcuffs together so that it's not too uncomfortable for you.' As he chatted on, he snapped one end round the bedpost and the fourth one round my wrist. I couldn't believe he was going to leave me handcuffed to the bed for two days. Involuntarily, I felt tears welling up in my eyes. In total panic I frantically blinked to force them back down. Unless Neil specifically requested it, crying wasn't normally allowed, and could bring about horrendous retribution. However, he very tenderly brushed the hair from my face and wiped away my tears with his fingers. He kissed me passionately as his hands caressed my naked body. I was trembling with fear and revulsion. I had wanted him to go, I couldn't stand him to be near me. Only moments earlier I was dreaming of my escape, but I was now overwhelmed with fear that he might not return and I would die shackled to this bed.

Neil said that if I was careful I could just about manage to use the potty he had left by the bedside. He'd left me one bottle of water a day – it wasn't much, but considering the weakness of my bladder and the awkwardness of the toilet arrangements he felt it was probably 'quite sensible'. He went on to inform me that he had cancelled the milk, then produced a torch which he said would be useful when I needed to wee, but not to leave it on or the batteries wouldn't last.

'I hope you have an interesting time. I want you to use it productively, darling. Think of how you can become a better, more loving and obedient wife, and all the different ways you can please me.'

His final gesture was to lock the bedroom door as he went out, but not before he had removed the light bulb from its fitting. Panic overwhelmed me as I heard the front door slam shut after him. Perversely, free at last to cry, my feeling of abandonment was such that I was now far beyond fear, way past tears. In total denial that this was actually happening, my mind became a battlefield of frantic arguments as to how and why I was here in the pitch-black room, abandoned and shackled to a bed.

I was supposed to be using this time to think about how I could become a better wife. I felt sick with fear.

I was fed up with my body and my mind reacting in the same cowardly way to Neil's cruelty and intimidation. I wanted to be brave and strong.

Why is it my fault? Why do I have to try harder? I don't love him any more; I hate him for treating me like this. Did I ever love him, or did I just want a knight in shining armour to rescue me? Well, that was the problem I suppose. Maybe I just wanted to be rescued and I thought I was in love, when really I wasn't. This was my punishment then, because if I really did love Neil I would be able to get everything right. It was probably because I didn't really love him that I'd made such a mess of everything. He was right, then; it was me who was all wrong.

If my head hadn't been so screwed up and confused, I wouldn't have made all the wrong decisions that resulted in me being handcuffed to the bed now. In actual fact, at this point in our relationship there was no need for locks, keys, handcuffs or restraints of any kind. I was far too cowed to have done anything practical about escaping. Oh, I spent a lot of my time dreaming about what my life might have been like if I hadn't met him. Escape plans were hatched weekly, daily, hourly, and as I lay on this bed, in the darkness, pretty well constantly.

In truth, I was far too afraid to make a break for it. What would Neil do to me should these plans fail? Or worse, should they succeed, and I escaped and he found me again? Neil had only to look at me a certain way, nod, place a hand lightly on my shoulder, and instantly I was alert to whatever he required of me. If he said stop, I stopped. If he ordered me to bring him the belt so that he could beat me with it, I brought him the belt, took the beating, and said thank you afterwards. Whatever Neil wanted, he got it, immediately; no arguments, no dirty looks, no non-compliant body language. Otherwise, the punishment was more severe than the original demand. The way to survive was to just do it, regardless of how awful it was, how demeaning, terrifying, painful or disfiguring. Switch off, go somewhere else, get it over with, at least until next time. Any resistance of any kind, even a twitch of the eyebrow, brought about the worst retribution imaginable, and it could go on for days.

As the minutes and hours slowly passed, I may have been hallucinating and delirious most of the time; I don't know. I was suffering from lack of food, not much water. I had no clock or watch; it was pitch black, I had no sense of time or space. My ears strained to make out any muffled sounds that might give me a clue about what time it was. For what seemed like hours, I listened for the milkman – but then remembered Neil had cancelled the milk. Something came through the letterbox; was it the post? Was it the first or the second day? I couldn't remember. I heard the distant sounds of front doors opening and closing, but were the people going to work or coming home after a long day? If only Neil hadn't put that blanket up over the curtains – not one chink of light came through the window. The bedroom door was closed and locked. If the torch battery gave out I'd be done for; I wouldn't even be able to see to have a wee.

So my thoughts and feelings chased each other around the room.

In the pitch-black darkness, the physical discomfort – muscle cramps, pins and needles, stiffness and cold – seemed to jockey for position with my sheer terror that, should Neil not return, this would be the slow and painful end of my life. This drove me almost to the point of madness. I began to have difficulty differentiating between sleeping and waking. Drifting in and out of each of these states, perhaps the only indication of which I was in was the degree of discomfort I was conscious of. By now I had completely lost track of time, unable to evaluate it any more.

In this trance-like state I only vaguely heard the sound of the key in the lock of the bedroom door. Then I became aware that Neil was standing over me. He was all fresh and smelling nice, standing there with his feet apart, arms crossed, looking coolly down at me, wearing what I think was meant to be a friendly smile. I was disorientated and I couldn't work out where I was, or how to react. I found it hard to make eye contact. My eyes were hurting trying to focus, and seemed to be darting all over the place. He was delivering one of his monologues, telling me how much he had missed me, loved me, the usual stuff. My mind wandered off a bit, and when I clicked back into the present I became aware that he was masturbating, saying something about my helplessness being a big turn-on, even though I did stink to high heaven. He ejaculated over my breasts and my face and, totally repulsed, I couldn't stop myself from retching.

I turned away from him, unable to stop my traitorous body from heaving and desperately trying to regurgitate the pitiful amount of water I had consumed over the last forty-eight hours. Clearly Neil was not expecting this reaction, and, grabbing me by the hair, he wrenched my head around.

'That is not quite how I expected to be greeted by my loving and obedient wife. So much for "absence makes the heart grow fonder". Obviously it sickens yours, you ungrateful bitch. I could have taped your mouth up and left you without water. I didn't have to leave your doggy blanket to keep you warm. But I did these things because I love you, because I'm kind, because I trust you – and do you appreciate it? No! And why don't you appreciate it? Because you are a spoilt bitch, that's why.'

'No Neil, please, I didn't realize it was you when you came in, please you've got to believe me. I didn't know if I was asleep or wandering, or what – I lost all track of time. I couldn't remember how long you had been gone and I was scared you had left me and you weren't coming back for me. I thought I was going to die handcuffed to this bed and you had abandoned me and noone would know I was here.' I began to sob uncontrollably and, unexpectedly, Neil sat down on the side of the bed and pulled me towards him. For the second time in two days he wiped away my tears with his fingers, then gripping my face in his hands, he forced me to make eye contact with him.

My already cold body began to freeze as I was forced to look into the icy blue depths of winter. The lips smiled around the perfect white teeth. 'You don't need to worry, sweetheart. "Till death us do part", remember? So, when I'm tired of you, when you no longer please me, I'll kill you. It'll be a much more amusing game than just abandoning you, handcuffed to a bed. You don't need to worry about it for a couple of years yet – I'm having a great time!'

I was rigid with fear. There was a lump in my throat but I couldn't swallow. My head was buzzing; I was shaking. My husband had just told me that he had every intention of killing me when he got bored with playing his sick games, and now it was as though nothing untoward had been said, and everything was back to what passed for normal in our relationship. It was too much for me to comprehend!

And now he was laughing, and being nice. He took the handcuffs off; massaged the torturous stiffness and soreness of my arm, shoulder and back muscles; ran me a bath with warm, scented water, bathed me, fed me; changed the bedding, tucked me into bed, got in beside me and fell asleep almost immediately. Eventually, through sheer nervous exhaustion, I fell into my normal restless sleep to be chased by monsters that were much less frightening than the one who lay peacefully asleep beside me.

So time passed. My days were filled with meticulous cleaning, washing, ironing, and cooking the meals, ready to be served exactly twenty minutes after Neil walked through the front door of his kingdom. This allowed him time to check that the flat had been cleaned to his standard and that all my tasks had been completed. I had an exercise regime to keep my body both in trim and supple. We had also started my dancing lessons.

Neil liked to play games; his latest game was dancing. I was quite a good dancer; when I was younger I used to go to ballet and tap-dancing classes, and I had performed in quite a few concerts. This wasn't quite the kind of dancing Neil had in mind, however. He was more interested in a mixture of modern dance, belly dancing and stripping. His contribution was to play hits from the Sixties on the record player. I had to dance for him in a suggestive and seductive way, which always ended up in me having to strip to the music. I would never be able to get this right for Neil. He would sit there with his belt in his hand, shouting instructions in order to be heard above the noise of the music. He would lash out with the belt, kick me up the backside every time I didn't perform as he wished. He was up and down off his chair like a jack in a box. What the neighbours must have thought, I have no idea. In the beginning I was convinced someone would come to complain about the noise, if nothing else. No one ever did. Slowly I just started to lose hope.

After our meal one evening, Neil announced we were going out. I began to feel apprehensive; he was up to something, but what was it? He had gone to the bedroom to choose my clothes. I followed him.

'Where are we going, Neil?'

'To this big pub in town to meet some mates. You'll like it, love, there's dancing. I'll just have a quick bath because you've already had one, haven't you? You get changed into one of these sexy little numbers. Can't wait for my mates to see you tonight.'

I wasn't sure I liked the sound of dancing. No, dancing didn't sound good to me, not at all. I examined the clothes on the bed – two scraps of lace for underwear, a dress that was so low at the front and so short that the top and the bottom almost met, at least that's how it seemed to me. Well, with any luck I would just fall off the shoes, which wouldn't be hard with the height of those heels. How to feel and look like a tart in fifteen minutes – sorry, thirty – Neil hadn't chosen the make-up and jewellery yet.

I had to admit it was nice to be out and pretending all was normal. In company Neil was good fun, and a charming and intelligent man. I had a drink and started to feel slightly more relaxed. When I asked him if I could go to the ladies he agreed that was a good idea, and said that when I came back I should start being nice to his friends. I had no understanding of what he meant by that, so I asked him. He told me to flirt with them, get them turned on, come on to them a bit, and then he wanted to see me dancing with them. I felt absolutely gutted and totally intimidated; I couldn't do it, I wouldn't. I told him I was married to him, I couldn't come on to other men. He grabbed me roughly by the arm and kind of frogmarched me to the ladies, smiling at me all the time. Outside the loo he told me I would do exactly as he wanted, or else.

'By the way,' he said, 'make sure the dancing is sensual and seductive, but you can keep your clothes on, this time.'

I sat on the toilet in the ladies in a blind panic. How on earth was I going to get out of this one? These blokes were all going to think I was a right slapper, but what could I do? I had no choice. I was too frightened not to do as Neil said. I stayed in the toilets as long as I dared, which wasn't too long as Neil was waiting outside for me.

'All right, babe?' He smiled at me as his arm snaked around my waist, pulling me in close. He bent over and whispered in my ear as we got near the bar: 'Better make this good entertainment for Daddy, or you know what to expect when I get you home, don't you?' He kissed my ear, patted my bottom, and gave me a gentle push in the small of my back towards the general direction of his friends.

I think there were about half a dozen of Neil's mates, all well into their fourth or fifth pint by now. I was counting my footsteps as I walked towards them, hoping for a personality transplant on the way. My tummy was full of butterflies and I was acutely aware that Neil was walking a discreet distance behind me.

Step one, couple of deep breaths.

Step two, shoulders back.

Step three, slight sway to the hips.

Step four, remember to breathe.

Step five, a bit of a pout to the lips.

Step six, big breath, even bigger smile, lean forward slightly, then . . .

'Hello, looks like the boys are having more fun than the girls. Mind if I join you?'

I was immediately surrounded by blokes. One got me a drink, another a cigarette, someone else lit it for me (I didn't smoke, but I smoked it anyway). Someone else told me a joke, which I can't remember it now but at the time I thought it was hysterically funny. Actually the whole thing was good fun. I didn't have to do anything – they were all falling over each other to be friendly, to get close to me, talk to me, and touch me (but not in an intimate way). I had another drink, my second of the evening, then I had another; three's my limit. One of the men asked me to dance, just as Neil joined the group.

'Okay to dance with the wife, Neil?'

'Be my guest. Hope you can keep up, she's a bit of a mover.'

Neil, realizing I was drunk, gave me a warning look. I guess I was too high on adrenalin and too pissed. I did take that look seriously – I felt a frisson of fear – but I wasn't terrified although I should have been.

I could say I wasn't sure how the rest of Neil's mates

got onto the dance floor, but I have a feeling I shouted over and invited them to join us. I guess the dancing lessons must have paid off, as I was really getting into the beat and the moves. The guys weren't really joining in, I felt, although they were doing a good job of keeping a space on the dance floor, forming a circle around me. I was starting to feel a bit weird; my head was spinning and I wasn't quite sure where I was. I closed my eyes; it was easier to concentrate on the beat that way. I was back in the front room hearing Neil shouting above the music, telling me to keep my arms moving, move my hips: 'Don't stand rooted to the spot, use the space, sway your body.' Vaguely I was aware of men clapping and whistling, and I thought, go for it girl. Then I was slipping the straps of my dress down my arms – whoops!

Mid dance my jacket was draped round my shoulders. Neil reached inside and without a word pulled the straps of my dress back up. He looked into my eyes, an icy blast hit my body, winter had arrived, and with it instant sobriety. He put his arm round my shoulders and turning back to his friends, invited them to join us both at the bar for a last drink. His friend Pete brought a barstool for me and Neil made a joke out of ordering me an orange juice, making sure everyone knew I couldn't hold my drink. When we said our goodnights, Neil's friends were all very chatty and friendly, and said they were looking forward to our next night out. Neil had the top of my arm in a grip of iron and it was all I could do not to scream out in agony.

On the way home the atmosphere in the cab was arctic.

'I'm sorry, Neil, I thought that was what you wanted. Isn't that what you wanted me to do? I only wanted to please you. I'm really sorry Neil. Please, don't be angry.' I was trying to sit up close next to him on the seat.

'Sit over there in the corner, darling, will you.' If he could overhear our conversation, the cab driver would never have guessed from Neil's pleasant, well-modulated voice that he was in the least put out. I, on the other hand, was thinking, oh fuck! Not a good sign, definitely not a good sign.

'Neil, I—'

'Let's just be quiet shall we, sweetheart? It's late and I expect we're both tired, aren't we?'

If I hadn't been to the toilet before we left the pub I think I would have wet myself through sheer terror.

By now the taxi had pulled up outside the flat, and unhurriedly he reached out and caught hold of my hand.

'Get out this side with me, love.' He held on to my hand until after he had paid the driver and the cab had driven off up the road. I watched the tail lights disappear into the darkness of the night, leaving me alone with Neil.

Chapter Seventeen

INVOLUNTARILY, MY FOOTSTEPS SLOWED as we turned right onto the garden path. It was about 11 p.m., and a clear, frosty autumn evening. I could hear the sound of my heart beating in my ears. My breathing quickened and became shallow, and my stomach began to cramp and my legs to shake. Like a cornered animal, I wanted to run, but there was no one and nowhere to run to, no escaping the inevitable. Neil put the key into the lock and we passed through the front door into the hall, into hell.

My feeling of dread was a sharp contrast to the warm, cosy glow cast by the lamp Neil had left burning on the table in the short, narrow hallway. I heard the door click quietly behind us, a light touch on my shoulder was my order to stop, and he reached around, unbuttoned my coat and took it from me.

'Turn around,' he said softly.

My blood ran cold and my legs turned to jelly. I tried hard to swallow down the panic rising through my body and threatening to escape up my throat and through my mouth as screaming, crying, begging, anything that might stop the nightmare replaying itself yet again. But I knew from bitter experience that any kind of emotion, unless requested by him and under his control, just made it worse for me.

I turned around slowly; he was leaning nonchalantly against the now locked and bolted front door, having removed his own outdoor coat. As usual, he looked the perfect up-to-the-minute stylish young man, from his black leather boots to his snazzy suit, shirt and tie – in blue, of course, to match his beautiful blue eyes.

The coldness of his eyes was doubly emphasized as he looked at me as if I had just crawled out from under the nearest stone, slowly shaking his head as he loosened his tie.

'I love you so much, and I try very hard to help you to be a good wife, but you just don't know how to behave, do you? You are such a low-life cunt, such a slag – you have no business being in the same room as ordinary decent people.'

His voice was grey monotone as he removed his tie and looped it around my neck, leading me down the hall to the second bedroom.

I did not resist – I was too frightened and resistance, I had learned from past experience, only made things worse. He continued his monologue, almost conversationally.

'Now I have to lose precious time when I should be sleeping, teaching you how to be obedient, how to behave in front of others. It's not that I mind that so much; after all, I do love you, so of course I want to help. My problem is, you never seem to learn, and next time we go out I can almost guarantee it will be exactly the same scenario. No – don't speak, I don't want to hear your miserable excuses. You're just a tart, a whore, and not a very intelligent one at that.'

As he half dragged me into the bedroom I could feel vomit rising into my throat and I started to retch. He looked at me with total contempt, ordered me to the toilet and settled himself in the easy chair in the bedroom.

How long can I make vomiting last? I'm not sure. I'm in a cold sweat, my head is hammering, I'm hot, I'm cold, what can I do?

A cold voice intruded through the fog of my panic: 'Teeth, then bedroom, bitch.'

I cleaned my teeth and somehow made my legs move forwards by concentrating on sliding one foot in front of the other, back into the bedroom. He was sitting where I had left him.

'Right, I've made my selection. I think I'm getting in the mood now; having to wait and think about you, and how you have misbehaved tonight, has helped,' he whispered in my ear, as he pulled me down onto his knee.

'Go and get handcuffs and the belt with the raised studs, then come into the lounge.'

He stood up with me in his arms, set me down on the floor, then lightly stroked the side of my face and kissed me on the lips and left.

I wanted to die. Why couldn't I just die? In the beginning I used to plan how I would escape. I could climb out of the window – it's a ground-floor flat – but he would hear me, and even if I got out of the window, he would catch me. I had no money so I wouldn't get far and if he caught me he would kill me. Dying would be okay, but it wouldn't be quick – he'd told me that. He would make it as painful as he could and make it last as long as he could. I had to try harder to be how he wanted me to be, and then it would be okay – it wouldn't be good, but it would be better than this!

'Put music on, then make me more comfortable darling. There's no reason why I shouldn't enjoy this. You should try and enjoy it too, look at it as being at school – learning ought to be fun.'

I can't believe the sick bastard. It must be him who's wrong, it can't be me, surely? I know I'm not perfect, but surely I don't deserve this. I know I might have done some bad things, but haven't I been punished for them?

I put some music on.

Very carefully and gently I started to undress him. There was an order, a way to do this, which I struggled to remember through my fear and loathing. Then came the part where I had to ask him to make love to me, and he says 'no', because I don't deserve him and I'm such a whore. At this point I don't know who I despised more; him for what he was doing to me, or myself for doing it.

Next came the striptease to the music. This was really hard, because I couldn't hear the beat of the music for my heart pounding in my ears; my legs wouldn't move as they were shaking like jelly. I waited, just waited, hardly daring to breathe; then all of a sudden a crack and a thud and a searing pain across my left breast signalled the beginning of my emotional withdrawal, thank God.

'I think you can do a bit better than that can't you, you fucking little shag bag. Let's find the beat for a start; let's get those hips moving, those legs, shoulders, arms. Come on, let's have some sex appeal, here's a bit of encouragement for you.'

The quiet voice could barely be heard above the sound of the music, the pounding of my heart, and the noise of the belt as it whacked against my skin, the raised studs drawing blood indiscriminately on my body, but not my face, not after the first time, and not until the very last time.

'That's better. After all, you proved earlier on tonight what a sexy dancer you are. Didn't you? I said, *didn't you?* No, don't speak just keep moving. I want to know why you are totally incapable of obeying me. Keep your clothes on this time, that's what I told you, you stupid bitch. You couldn't even get that right, could you? It's not that you can't get things right, you just don't want to. You're disobedient, a bad person, a useless wife. You like humiliating me in front of my friends. That's why you have to be punished. Dance to the beat, just keep the beat. Move, keep moving.'

By this point I had learned to hide the real Nikola away when he beat me. It's as if I was up in the corner of the room, watching the part of me that was being abused. I knew it was happening but I could only vaguely feel it. Somehow, I had turned the feeling switch down by thinking about my dad when I was a little girl. I was remembering when I was three or four in that pre-fab flat, when my dad used to pee into the enamel bucket and always used to sing 'I'm Forever Blowing Bubbles' to mask the noise. So what was really happening was a bit like this:

'Dance to the beat, just keep the beat, move, keep moving.'

(I'm forever blowing bubbles, pretty bubbles in the air . . .)

'Move your hips, move your legs, shoulders, arms.'

(They fly so high, nearly reach the sky, then like my dreams they fade and die . . .)

'Come on let's have some sensuality.'

After a while, in spite of not wanting to, I would come back into the room, or into reality, if you like. What I could never really understand was the way he seemed rather amused at my suffering and humiliation.

'Come here,' he said. 'I like to see you naked and bleeding. Sit on my lap while I fuck you like the bitch you are. Crawl.'

I don't know how I even managed to crawl across the lounge floor. I know when I sat on top of him and he forced himself inside me it burned and hurt and I cried and begged him to stop. He bit my nipple and made it bleed, and then he told me never to cry or beg because it turned him off and that meant death for me. This wasn't new; he had told me this before, but some-times the pain was too much! After he'd climaxed, in a very patient voice he explained that it was his job to control me, but that I had to learn to control myself.

Oh God! If you are up there, or out there, or any-where, kill him, or me, and make it quick, please; or even just send me mad, so I don't know what's happening, or I can't feel anything, please.

He's kissing and stroking me now. Why, what's happening? Everything hurts, I hurt everywhere – please let me die. I don't want to be here anymore. Then: 'Bring me your handcuffs, darling.'

What new madness is this? I thought it was over, at least for tonight, for this time. Please, let it at least be over for now.

'Do I have to ask twice? I hope not. I did think we were getting somewhere at last.' His voice was full of disappointment.

Once again I was no longer in my body. I felt distanced from myself, as though I was watching myself being punished for something which I may or may not have done. I had now lost all perspective, all grip on reality, temporarily at least. I am bad, I must be.

I saw myself bring him the handcuffs and follow him into our bedroom. He handcuffed me to the bed by my wrists then went to the bathroom, coming back with a razor blade.

His patience was truly wonderful as he explained how he would brand me now, so no other man would ever want to look at me. He was forced to do this, he said, because I was so promiscuous, and could not be trusted around other men. He then proceeded to cut me in the area between my pubic hair and just above my navel, not very deeply, but just enough to scar me. He explained, yet again very patiently, that he'd just do it a few at a time.

'Just a few each time, just enough for you to cope with. See how much I love you? I'm always thinking about you.'

Afterwards, he bathed me, stuck white sticky tape on my wounds, and told me he was hoping for an improvement in my behaviour in the future. He then asked me to put clean sheets on the bed while he had a bath.

Dad, Mum – Oh God, somebody – please help me, save me, kill me, do something. Why can't I just die?

Chapter Eighteen

I WAS SPENDING MORE AND more of my time on some other level in a desperate attempt to escape reality. I would sit down to drink a cup of coffee, my mind racing round like a rat in a trap desperately seeking some means of escape from my situation. Two hours later – my coffee cold in my cup and my limbs stiff and aching, having been locked in the same position for too long – I would return from this futile exercise, my mind exhausted, my tasks for the day only half finished. I would have achieved nothing except to add to my panic and stress levels by rushing around like someone demented to get everything done and save myself another beating, or worse.

This was how I spent my lonely days, including my wedding anniversary. Needless to say, there was no question of Neil and I exchanging cards or marking the occasion in any normal way. I was hurting so badly from the previous night's beating that I could hardly move and yet I forced my aching body to clean the house, finishing all the tasks Neil had told me to do before he arrived home. I spent the day dreading Neil's threatened anniversary present of exquisite pain and humiliation. What did it mean and how would I survive? I cannot bear to write about what he did to me that night. But survive I did, night after night.

In her letters to me, my mother had repeatedly suggested that she came for a visit. It worried me that Neil would refuse permission for her to come. It would have meant collecting her in the car and taking her back and it was a long drive. Every time she asked I was torn between hope and despair. Hope that maybe she would rescue me and despair that she would see what was happening and walk away. I had never been able to trust her to take care of me when I was a child, why should things be any different now?

Not long after our wedding anniversary I realized that my period was late. I desperately tried to deny the possibility that I was pregnant, hiding away from the calendar and the little red dot Neil put there every month. I knew he would be aware I was late. I just wasn't sure why he hadn't mentioned it yet. The knowledge hadn't influenced him to let up on the sex and violence and my stomach, thanks to his skilful wielding of Mr Razor Blade, now looked surprisingly similar to spaghetti junction. Certainly I didn't want to bring a baby into this relationship. The thought of a child having to witness what Neil was doing to me, or having to endure a similar experience itself — well, no way. It just wasn't going to happen. I had to do something, but I didn't know what yet.

One evening Neil was playing his puppy game. I was kneeling between his legs, sitting on my heels with my back to him. He was listening to smoochy music, leaning forwards slightly over my shoulders massaging my breasts and midriff with baby oil from behind. He kissed the top of my head and said, 'Daddy's made puppy pregnant. It looks as though my fun and games may have to be curtailed for a while. I guess we'll have to get your body cleaned up for your visit to the doctor's. How long might that take do you think? Hmmm. I'm not sure myself. Bruises and cuts don't take too long. Cigarette burns, well there aren't too many of those, some of them are just singes really aren't they, babe? Mr Razor's been a bit of a naughty boy though hasn't he? Still, I reckon in about three or four months they'll just look like stretch marks. So if you're a good girl you'll be able to go and see the doctor when you're about four months. What do you think?'

'Well, I'm sure if that's what you think, you'll be right, Neil.' I had to keep reminding myself that although this was my life, it was not normal; that normal people did not have conversations like the one we had just had. My husband was not okay, he couldn't be, surely he was crazy, wasn't he?

'This would be a good time for your mother to visit then, don't you think? If your master has to deprive himself he may as well have extra reasons to be on his best behaviour. Shall we arrange that, puppy?'

I couldn't quite trust him, was this part of the game? 'If that's what you want, Neil. I just want to please you.' I had learned how to grovel very well, but that didn't mean I liked it. I was sick with humiliation. I didn't want to please him, I wanted to kill him, but I was too scared.

He told me to write to my mum and invite her to come and stay in about a month's time for two weeks. It was a long way and he would prefer not to have to drive on two consecutive weekends. He made a big show of inspecting my body. 'You should be okay by then, provided you behave yourself, do as you're told. Let's not forget, darling, if you were a proper and obedient wife you wouldn't have to be punished. If you weren't so persistently feckless, I wouldn't get so bored with the whole tedious business of making you into my kind of wife. If you would just comply, submit to my control, if you only really loved me – well, then I wouldn't have to resort to playing games in order to keep myself interested enough to help you. I love you so much and I'm never going to give up on you, I want you to know that.'

Like an animal I could smell his sexual arousal, but also my own fear. I had heard him pronounce what felt to me like my death sentence. He touched me, flicked my nipple, and immediately I disappeared out of my body, upwards to touch the ceiling where I hugged myself, keeping safe. I was finding it much easier as time went on to detach myself from myself. My dad sang to me then and somewhere in the room below a monster savaged my body. I could hear him vaguely in the distance calling me horrible names, ordering me to do things to pleasure him. I could taste his semen in my mouth, choking and gagging as he made me swallow it.

Maybe, just maybe, there was a small glimmer of light. My mum was coming and perhaps somehow I could now affect a means of escape. If I couldn't have the courage for myself, perhaps I could find the strength from somewhere within me to save my unborn child.

I watched myself being led around the room by my collar and lead on my hands and knees. Neil hit me on my back and bottom with his belt. He tied my lead to the chair leg as he fucked me from behind but I couldn't really feel it. Puppy was hurting and really frightened and I did feel sad for her. I was on the ceiling, floating, relaxing, Dad was singing:

'I'm forever blowing bubbles, pretty bubbles in the
air,

They fly so high, nearly reach the sky,

Then like my dreams they fade and die.

Fortune's always hiding, I've looked everywhere,

I'm forever blowing bubbles, pretty bubbles in the
air.'

I said thanks to Dad, and it was okay now, time for
bath and bed. Neil laid me down gently on the bed,
kissed me tenderly on the mouth and slipped into bed
beside me. He was telling me how beautiful and precious
I was as he kept stroking me, moulding my body against
him. It was cloying, suffocating, I started to feel hot and
panic-stricken. Stop it, stop it, I kept saying to myself
over and over again. Calm down, deep breaths, control
yourself, don't let him see how frightened, how fragile
you feel. Just lie still, don't move, not even an eyebrow.
I pretended I was a statue, until eventually my nightmares
took over.

Neil enjoyed his sick sexual games and the power and
control he exerted over me. It was a pointless exercise
trying to get everything right for him. He didn't want me
to, what would be the fun in that? I was now in an agony
of despair – no longer able to believe or buy into his
story that he loved me, that it was all for my own good

and to improve our relationship; that it was all my fault and I was a bad person. This last phrase was like a mantra he kept re-enforcing in my head. I was no longer able to decipher whether this statement was true, in that I believed it myself or not. I did believe he must be mad and he was trying to send me mad. I was aware that I was slowly going out of my mind and I knew I had to do something soon. Eventually he would take over my will to survive, even my thoughts, controlling me totally. I was dangerously near that point now. In desperation I was pinning my hopes on my mother.

Over the last four weeks Neil's use of physical abuse had been kept to a minimum although the sexual abuse continued and the emotional abuse increased as he found new ways to humiliate me. He was very sad, he said, to have to empty the wardrobe in the spare bedroom and pack away his 'toys', but my relief was very hard to conceal from him. Even after the box was locked in the garden shed, I was expecting him to laugh and say 'only joking, didn't mean it, bring me your handcuffs'. Surprisingly he didn't and that felt like a kind of freedom.

On the journey 'back home' to collect Mum and my youngest brother Joe I was treated to a monologue on being an obedient and dutiful wife. It was the usual stuff again: don't show him up, don't let him down, how he was putting all his trust in me. My mum and Joe were there for two weeks and I had to be on my best behaviour, loving, caring, thoughtful towards him. He wanted me to be romantic, happy, upbeat, blah, blah, blah, on and on and on. I just kind of put my listening, attentive 'you know everything, you are always right, you are God' face on and tuned out eventually. All my senses had been blunted and I didn't really feel things in the same way now.

We travelled home late afternoon one Friday and stayed until the Sunday. It was so good to see friends and relatives and have a break. However, I was a bit concerned about my youngest brother Joe who was coming back with us. He was about eight, quiet and rather nervous and shy. I hoped Neil wasn't going to kick off while Mum and Joe were there. James, who was nearly ten years old, was staying at home with my nana and Dad. He was a much tougher proposition altogether, with an unpredictable temper. We were very close and had he witnessed any of my abuse, I know his reaction would have been to launch himself at Neil and do his utmost to defend me. A child is no match for a man though, especially someone like Neil. Not only was he extremely violent, but my own experience had taught me, he also had no human compassion whatsoever.

Before we left on the Sunday I hugged my dad extra

tight. He had no idea how he had unwittingly helped me through the past months.

Neil had been his usual charming self all weekend and this continued on the journey back to the flat even though my mum was a difficult travelling companion. She couldn't go anywhere on her own and, like a small child, insisted everyone took constant care of her. However, even her weak bladder, frequent toilet breaks and her insistence that I accompany her and Joe to the toilet didn't disturb Neil's equilibrium.

It was a long journey, the traffic was heavy and we were all exhausted by the time we reached the flat. After relaxing with a very welcome cup of tea, Neil announced that he was going to the local fish and chip shop. He said he wasn't having his pregnant wife cooking when she was tired. My insides curled with distaste and I wanted to vomit as my mum praised him for being so thoughtful. It was on the tip of my tongue to remind Neil it was Sunday and the chip shop was closed, but I'm positive he would have remembered that. Neil never did anything without thinking about it and weighing it up first. I wasn't surprised when he came back pretending to look all sad and upset – yeah, that'll be right, I was thinking to myself as I offered to make bacon and eggs.

As we got into bed later that evening I heard Mum

telling Joe what a nice flat it was and how lucky I was to be living there. Neil was so knackered he fell asleep almost immediately. As I lay beside him I ruminated on how lucky I was. Well I had spent the weekend without being abused – that was lucky, I suppose. I did have to ask permission to get up in the mornings and go to the toilet and Neil had still told me what to wear and what to eat, except for the bacon and eggs I had cooked for supper tonight, but those rules had become a part of the fabric of my life and I accepted them as normal. So, as I drifted off to sleep, I decided that the last couple of days had been very lucky for me.

Neil went to work on Monday. He told me I had to make the bed, wash the dishes, keep the flat tidy and make a meal *but* I didn't have to clean. I was allowed to wear proper clothes, not tart's clothes! He gave me money! I was allowed to go out! I could take Mum and Joe wherever they wanted to go! We could go shopping! We could eat whatever we wanted for tea! I could take Mum and Joe next door for coffee! We could go for a walk!

I was really excited. I felt free, and I didn't know what to do first. I wanted to do everything all at once. Mum told me to slow down and said she came for a rest not to go rushing off doing everything at once. Then she reminded me I was pregnant and ought to be taking things easy.

'Anybody would think you never got out anywhere. What do you normally do on Mondays?' She was laughing as she plonked herself down at the kitchen table with her second cup of tea and a cigarette. I was sure she wouldn't want to hear the absolute truth about how I really spent my days. Before he left that morning, Neil had warned me what would happen to me should I be tempted to tell his secrets.

'Mondays I would normally just spend cleaning, Mum. You know how men are, make a mess wherever they go. After the weekend the flat always looks as though a bomb's hit it.'

By the time we had washed the dishes and made the beds the decision about how to amuse ourselves had been taken out of our hands by Joe. He wanted to go to the park, so the park it was – then food shopping. We spent a pleasant day just being 'normal'. After Neil came home, we drank a couple of glasses of wine, chatted and watched television, just like other people do. It felt great. To me it was 'normal'.

Because Neil had an audience, he once again reverted to that other charming, pleasant, intelligent, likeable person. The monster from the deep was kept well hidden, even in the privacy of our bedroom. In our most intimate moments he became the tender, amorous lover. Still there was the occasional 'I didn't say you could go to the toilet yet' or 'did you ask permission to leave my bed' on the odd occasion when I did actually forget. And although my clothes were normal, not tarty, Neil was still choosing them every day. If it hadn't been for these timely reminders I would have begun to believe I had imagined everything else, that it was me who was crazy.

Bit by bit I began to relax and I suppose that's when I made my big mistake. Perhaps I had started to believe that everything was going to be all right – I'm not sure now.

On the tenth day of Mum's holiday Neil was late home. Neil was a very precise person – if he wasn't going to be home until four minutes past six that's what time he would say he would be home. Meals had to be on the table twenty minutes after he walked through the door, not nineteen, not twenty-one, but twenty – or else. Neil said he would be home at six o'clock and the meal was ready at exactly six twenty, but he had not arrived. I was in a quandary about what I should do and I began to feel scared. Those fears so recently buried but just below the surface came shooting back into my consciousness. My mother, used to my dad's long absences at the pub, and totally unaware of any undercurrents, suggested we eat.

Mum and Joe ate their meal; I couldn't eat anything. It was so totally out of character for Neil not to do exactly what he said he was going to do. Had he had an accident? I was totally confused. I didn't understand what had happened. Eventually I decided to try and push the anxiety away, to carry on as normal for Mum and Joe. After all, in the outside world of 'normality', husbands going to the pub or being late home from work happened all the time.

After supper, I washed the dishes while Joe dried – but under protest. Mum said he had to help and I was making it into a game to make the time go faster. We were singing our version of some daft song at the tops of our voices, dive-bombing the cutlery in and out of the water, when I sensed a movement behind me. For a split second I heard a whooshing noise, felt a dull pain, then everything went black.

According to Mum, Neil appeared in the kitchen door-
way and took one look at me and Joe. In one continuous movement he walked from the doorway to the sink, picking up the breadboard on the way, and smacked me hard on the back of the head with it. Mum said I just dropped to the floor like a stone, unconscious. She thought I was only out for a few seconds. When I came round Neil was kicking me repeatedly in the base of my spine and calling me all kinds of filthy names, giving me a row about singing in the house without his permission.

He was saying something about going out to buy a cot for our baby, then coming back to the house and finding me singing and flaunting myself with my fucking free-loading family. He wasn't shouting though, he was saying it calmly and quietly. After every couple of words he would kick me. Mum was trying to stop him, while Joe cried and cringed by the sink.

My head felt funny, full of cotton wool, dizzy. It was hurting and I felt sick, but I knew I had to get Mum and Joe away from Neil.

'Mum, Mum, listen, take Joe and go into the bed-room. Go *now*. Please Mum, please, please, go now.'

Mum wasn't really listening – she was too wound up and scared. 'Neil, stop that right now. Have you forgotten she's pregnant? What on earth's the matter with you, have you gone mad?' Mum was shaking now. My dad could lash out after a drink and give her a backhander, but I knew she had never experienced anything like this.

'Living with your fucking daughter's enough to make anybody go mad, I'll tell you. You don't know the half of it. I'm going for a drink. I don't want her in my bed tonight, tell her that will you please, Mum. Sorry, didn't mean to upset you, sorry Joe.'

I hadn't seen him arrive, I didn't see him leave. I had tried to sit up but my vision was blurred and I was very dizzy. I was anxious to make everything seem all right again, for Joe especially but also for Mum who was patently worried about me. She brought a cold flannel and a drink of water, and eventually I was able to drag myself up off the kitchen floor. My back was really hurting, as was my head. I managed to get as far as the spare bedroom and collapsed on one of the beds. Mum brought me painkillers and I kept drifting in and out of either sleep or consciousness. At some point I must have got undressed and back into bed again. Joe slept with my mum in the other single bed.

During the night Neil came into the room. I could smell that he had been drinking. He said he'd come to apologize, he hadn't known what had come over him, he was really sorry, it wouldn't happen again. He told me how much he loved me, the usual stuff. Then he leaned over the bed to kiss me and whispered in my ear, 'They'll be gone soon, then who's going to protect you? Don't think you won't be sorry, you will be. Believe me, you're going to be very sorry indeed.' In his normal voice he wished me goodnight, sleep tight.

I didn't sleep much after that, and what sleep I had was broken by even more ghoulish nightmares than usual. Giant razor blades were ripping open my stomach and slashing at my baby. Large hands were forcing open my vagina, pulling my child out by its head, then ripping it off and feeding it to a dragon breathing fire.

The next morning Neil had gone to work before I could force open my eyes and face the day, my mother and her inquisition. She, however, had not been asleep when Neil got up and he had made the most of this opportunity. He told Mum he'd been having real problems with me and was beginning to think he had made a huge mistake. I was wild, a flirt, totally unpredictable. If she didn't believe him, she could talk to some of his mates. He was ashamed to take me out. Only the other week he'd taken me to a pub where there was dancing. I had shown him up by behaving like a tart. Drunk as a skunk, I'd taken all his friends onto the dance floor and proceeded to dance for them. Not with them, for them. It was disgusting, he told my mother. He had got to me just as I'd started to take my dress off. He'd been so embarrassed in front of his friends, and they all felt really sorry for him. He had asked her to have a word with me, get me to sort myself out!

As she told me this I was gobsmacked. The bastard, the clever, conniving, manipulative bastard. What now, I thought to myself. If I tell her the truth about what's actually been happening, will she believe me – would anyone? If I hadn't lived it myself, experienced it, would I? In all honesty, no I wouldn't. I would never have believed anyone could treat another human being the way I had been treated. My mum wasn't big on the loyalty stakes, she wasn't the brightest of people. In her own way she really loved me, but she was no match for Neil. I didn't know what to do next.

So, I compromised and told her a version of the truth. That Neil was unpredictable and unreasonable and the relationship at times was violent. She had to know that was true – she'd witnessed it herself. Even so, she found it hard to believe that Neil liked me flirting with his mates and that it had just got a bit out of hand that night. I stopped there – if she found that hard to believe, I couldn't see the point in telling her any more. My back was really sore and I was having pain low down at the front. I wasn't feeling well and went back to bed.

I decided staying in bed was a good idea and took more painkillers with my tea and toast. My head was a lot better but occasionally I felt a bit woozy. I slept most of the day. Neil came in to see me as soon as he got in from work and sat on the bed stroking the hair back from my face, all loving concern. Would I like another pillow, a hot water bottle, something to eat? I shook my head no, as I thought, fuck off bastard.

'Mum was thinking she might go tomorrow evening instead of the following morning. What do you think, babe? Think you'll be well enough to travel?'

I shrugged. How the hell was I supposed to know that? Here were two people who both professed to 'really love me' yet neither of them had suggested I should see a doctor. Neil decided they would wait and see how I was. I did sleep most of the night. As I drifted in and out of consciousness I heard everyone laughing and joking, voices on the television, smelled food cooking but I wasn't aware of Neil coming to bed. When I woke in the morning he was there, beside me, looking at me coldly.

'Well,' equally chilly, 'how's the patient?'

'I need to go to the toilet please, Neil,' I said with as much dignity as I could muster.

'Hurry up, then. I have to go to work soon and I need to know what's happening tonight.'

I hadn't thought I was going to be able to walk to the bathroom without being doubled over in agony but I wasn't too bad. My head was much better and my back, although bruised, was now merely a nagging ache. The pains low down at the front had gone, at least for the moment. I relayed this information to Neil who decided I was well enough to travel later that afternoon. He gave me a list of what to pack but told me not to do any cleaning. 'You need to rest and look after my baby. I don't want you doing anything else to put my child at risk, do you understand?' As I nodded my head in agreement I was thinking, this guy is totally unbelievable. He just looked at me – I knew he had read my mind and that was something else I was going to regret.

I spent the day working on my mother. Unfortunately I was becoming as manipulative as Neil. I played on the violence she had witnessed, Neil's unpredictability and my pregnancy and fears that something was going to happen to the baby. We had a debate that lasted most of the day – she was not an easy person to win over. We covered: Why get pregnant in the first place? Why get married in the first place? My so-called drink problem. My flightiness and wildness, both borne out by my hippy lifestyle which 'poor Neil' knew nothing about 'thank God', according to my mother. Eventually she agreed she would speak to Dad and try to persuade him to let me stay at home.

My heart was full of joy. Surely my dad who loved me dearly, his best and favourite child, his beautiful little girl, surely he wouldn't deny me the safety and security of my own home? Not when Mum told him what she had witnessed, not when Joe confirmed it and how much it had scared him. My dad would take care of me, he would protect me, that's what dads did.

In spite of the dull ache at the bottom of my spine and low down at the front I could barely conceal my high spirits as we packed up the car late that afternoon.

Even after all Neil's best efforts to manipulate my mother, she was going to help me. I was going to escape. I could almost taste my freedom. The car couldn't go fast enough for me.

'For heaven's sake, Mum, not another wee, surely. It's only just over half an hour since you had the last one. I'm glad you haven't passed your weak bladder on to the only daughter in the family.'

It seemed like a long way home that time.

Chapter Nineteen

BACK AT MY PARENT'S house, I was worried that the pains in my back and low down at the front still seemed to come and go. Nobody mentioned that I should be seen by a doctor and I couldn't understand this lack of concern. Neil went to visit his mum alone. As I wasn't ordered to go, I assumed he didn't want her giving me the third degree about why I wasn't feeling well.

While Neil was out, Mum told Dad about what happened. He was sitting in his favourite armchair, elbows on the arms, hands under his chin, legs crossed and with a face like thunder. 'He did what?' Dad shouted, then I heard Mum's slightly quieter voice continuing with her story. I was in the room and listening, but not really paying attention, like a child letting the adults' conversations float over her head. I was so sure of the outcome. Then Dad said he thought I should go back and try to make the marriage work, one last time, maybe just for a month.

'I can't, Dad, you don't understand what he's like.'

But he wasn't listening to me. He kept saying I had to think about the baby, that the baby had to be taken into consideration.

'If you weren't pregnant then you could stay at home, no problem,' he said. 'But you are, so you have to give it one last try. If it doesn't work then you can come home. If you won't give it one last try, you can't come home. You've made your bed and you'll just have to lie on it, that's my last word on the subject.'

'And what if he kills me Dad, or the baby?'

'Don't be so bloody melodramatic.'

I was totally crushed. In the space of twenty-four hours I had gone from believing that freedom was virtually round the corner to seeing it snatched from right under my nose. To make matters worse, earlier, after Neil had said he was going to visit his mum, he had told me to have a rest because I looked dreadful. I had used that excuse to say I was going to stay at Mum and Dad's 'until I felt better'. I was glad now that I hadn't been stupid enough to actually say I was leaving him. Even so, he had just looked at me and walked out.

At this point I'm not sure what was more frightening, having to go back with Neil, or the actual pain I was going through and its implications for the baby. I told Mum and she said that it was nature's way. If something was wrong with the baby, then I would mis-carry and nothing could be done about that at this early stage in the pregnancy. There was no point in going to the doctor, he wouldn't do anything, just let nature take its course.

I begged Dad not to send me back with Neil, told him Neil thought I was staying with them. 'If you send me back now, I'm going to get a good hiding for this. Don't you understand, he's going to beat me with a belt. Not just with his hand. Not even with just his fist. Dad, please. I think he might kill me, Dad!'

My dad had total confidence in his ability to put the fear of God into anybody. All of my objections were swept to one side with the reassurance that he would speak to Neil, and there was no way he would dare to lay a finger on me after that. True to his word, Dad spoke to Neil for about an hour before we set off. Half the road could hear him shouting, threatening what he would do to him if he ever laid a finger on his daughter in anger again. Neil's voice, on the other hand, was calm and quiet but he also had plenty to say. If his chat with my mum was anything to go by, this conversation would also be full of manipulative bullshit.

There are no words to describe how I felt when I left my parents' house. I had arrived on Friday evening full of hope, believing I had affected my escape. I was leaving on Sunday, and it felt to me as though it was probably to go to my death. I could only pray it would be quick. Well, I wouldn't pray, I didn't believe in God any more. God was a man too!

On Saturday, after Dad told me I had to go back I had written a letter to Chrissie while Neil was still out. James had posted this letter for me, not knowing that under the rules it wasn't allowed. Chrissie was now a student nurse. I had asked her if she knew of any way I could bring on a miscarriage, if there were some tablets I could take or that she could get me. I didn't want my baby to be killed violently by Neil, kicked to death, thumped, stabbed, whatever. If there is a God, let me at least help my baby die peacefully before he tortures me to death!

Neil never spoke to me at all during the long journey back to the flat. He didn't look at me, nor acknowledge me in any way whatsoever. He stopped once, for a toilet break, and when I got back to the car Neil was already waiting. He set off again without a single word. I was left with my own thoughts and fears. Did I believe anything my dad had said to Neil would stop him from doing exactly what he wanted with me? No. My mind could not even begin to contemplate the horror of what was to come. Eventually I blotted it out with sleep.

I was awakened by the car engine being switched off.

We were there. Neil lit a cigarette, rubbed the back of his neck, closed his eyes, and took a couple of long, deep drags. I scarcely dared to breathe as I tried to watch him covertly from the corner of my eye. He flicked his cigarette out of the car window, turned and smiled at me with all the charm of a deadly rattlesnake. He was out of the car in a flash muttering something about getting the show on the road. He had the suitcase out of the boot, my car door open, his hand under my elbow, and was steering me up the garden path before I'd even collected my thoughts. We had just got into the flat and he had dumped the suitcase in the hall when he remembered he hadn't locked up the car. That's unusual, I thought to myself amidst all my conflicting emotions. He was just going to lock the car he was saying and yes, before I asked, I could go to the loo.

Thankfully, I escaped to the bathroom. The pains in my back and front had eased off quite a bit again, probably with resting on the journey I was thinking as I sat on the toilet.

'Come out, come out, wherever you are.' His voice sounded playful, but I was startled; I hadn't heard him come back in. I jumped off the loo in a total panic, struggling to pull my knickers up. Shit, what now – the voice didn't go with his wintry expression. It was a game, but what was happening? What was he going to do now? What should I do? A scream escaped from my throat as the bathroom door suddenly burst open! He sprinted across the floor, grabbed hold of me, clamped his mouth over mine, and stuck his tongue down my throat. Shoving me back down on the toilet he said he hoped I had enjoyed him kissing me, as it was the only kiss I was getting tonight. He had not the slightest interest in putting his lips, tongue or even his dick anywhere near the mouth of a lying little trollop like me. All the time he was talking he was using the bathroom scissors to cut a strip of thick, grey, sticky tape off a roll.

'I'm glad I remembered this tape was in the car. Otherwise I may have had to listen to even more of your fucking lies. Now I won't.' He stuck the tape over my mouth. 'I want you to know, that unlike other occasions that have been painful to me and I have not enjoyed . . .' he started, ripping my clothes from my body. I put up my hands defensively, to stop him. He slapped my face. 'You should know better than that, don't ever try to stop me from taking my pleasure. Now, where was I . . . ?' He used the scissors to cut the waistband of my skirt, then ripped it from my body. 'After my conversation with your father today, I really am going to enjoy tonight. I just want you to know that, okay? Nod your head if you understand.'

I nodded my head. 'Good, now we can take our time, savour every moment.' Slowly, he removed the rest of my clothes, then his own. When he took the belt out of his jeans, I wet myself. He laughed. He kept laughing all the time he was beating me. He kept repeating everything my dad had said to him. After a while I didn't feel it so much and it wasn't important. It was sad though, because my dad didn't sing for me that night. I was alone on the ceiling watching myself. It was hurting quite a lot more without Dad to keep me safe.

Eventually Neil got bored with hitting me. Or maybe his arm just got tired. He masturbated over my breasts and left me on the floor in the hall. He said to stay there, he didn't want me anywhere near him because I was a lying piece of trash. I didn't want to be with him but I was cold, and I was hurting all over. I wanted my dad and my mum.

Why doesn't anybody want to help me, am I so horrible, so outrageously awful? Do I really, honestly deserve this?

I managed to fall asleep even though I was lying on the hard hall floor. I woke up once, feeling my cold body hurting all over, but I was grateful to Neil for having removed the tape from my mouth. I remember wondering when he did that, before I slipped back into the terrors of my usual nightmares.

When I came back to full consciousness I was aware that Neil was standing over me. It must be morning. I lay perfectly still, my eyes closed. Maybe he would just go to work and leave me. I should have known better by now.

'Take a bath – you stink, bitch.' The hairs on the back of my neck stood up as I recognized his normal, conversational tone. I think it was his coldness, his lack of compassion that made me know, somewhere deep inside me, that one day he would kill me. More than that, I thought he would enjoy it. He would certainly believe I deserved it.

It was a struggle to get up off the floor, I was so stiff and sore. The pain in my back and front was there most of the time now. At least that's how it felt, it was hard to tell as everywhere else hurt so much. I think my skin was broken in places from the belt the night before. The bath helped; it warmed me up, stopped me aching so much. Neil came into the bathroom just as I finished cleaning my teeth. I flinched as he came up behind me and stared into my eyes in the mirror over the sink. He took me by the shoulders, turned me round and started to inspect my body, running his hands over it, looking at the damage he had caused. I felt like an animal at the vet's.

'Hmmm. Not quite ready for round two yet. That's a shame. You'd better stay in bed today and rest, give your body time to heal. Off you go.'

I exited the bathroom as quickly as my painful body would allow me to, not quite believing I had been dismissed so easily, and crawled gratefully into bed. Neil had followed me into the bedroom with a glass of milk and some tablets. My orders were that I wasn't to get out of bed. The tablets were to help with the pain and the milk was for his baby. I wasn't allowed anything to eat. I started to protest; I hate milk, and he knew I hated milk. Even the smell of it makes me feel sick.

When I was four I had my tonsils removed and the first thing the nurse gave me afterwards was a cup of milk to drink. I told her I hated milk but she made me drink it anyway. I was immediately sick all over the bed, and myself, and the nurse was cross. Neil stood by the side of the bed and made me drink the glass of milk and take the tablets. Silent tears ran down my cheeks. I was retching, choking; all he did was make fun of me.

'Oh, those poor little puppy dog eyes, so sad,' he was laughing. 'Come on, stop messing about, hurry up and drink it. I'm not being late this morning for a no good, lying little tart like you.' He took the glass from me and disappeared to the kitchen. On his way out he poked his head round the bedroom door and intoned in a soft, menacing voice, 'I'll leave you with this thought, puppy. If my baby dies, so do you. See you later.'

A few months earlier, maybe even a few weeks, that

threat would have sent me into a paroxysm of fear. My body would have gone into adrenalin overload as panic set in. But my senses and emotions were now so blunted by everything I had experienced, my body now so used to experiencing pain, that my first reaction was . . . relief, in a way. At least it was going to be over. At last there would be an end.

His baby was going to die. I knew it, and I could feel it dying inside me. It didn't feel like part of me, not any more. I'd had no say in choosing whether I should have a child. It had not been conceived in a loving relationship; it was part of him. If it should survive, could I love it? Yes, it was part of me too – but what if it was just like him? What if the baby survived and he treated it the same way he treated me? No, I just couldn't bear it. Better that we both die, the baby first, then me.

I was scared about his continual threats to kill me. I took them seriously; he meant them. He would call it his dying game. I knew it would be long, slow and painful. Part of me thought, bring it on, do your worst, it doesn't matter any more. It worried me a bit that Dad was no longer with me to help me through the pain, but I would manage somehow. I had to, didn't I? While I was practising singing our song to myself, I think I was so comforted I fell asleep. Mercifully, I slept on and off all day. I woke up just after Neil had come home, and I heard him in the bathroom.

After he flushed the toilet, I heard him go into the kitchen. Then he shouted through and told me I could go. Thank God for that, I said to myself as I shuffled through to the bathroom feeling as stiff as an old woman. He appeared at the bathroom door.

'You can go back to bed when you've finished in here. I've decided for the sake of my baby I'd better feed you. Think yourself lucky.'

I hardly heard him. The cramping pains kept coming and I had a constant heavy, dragging feeling low down at the front. I wished it could be all over.

I must have dozed off again because I never heard Neil come in, but suddenly he was standing beside the bed, holding a tray. Presumably there was food on the tray, I couldn't see from where I was. All I could see from my prone position on the bed was the top half of a glass. Please, God, not more milk! He was telling me to sit up. Warily I sat up – chicken salad and orange juice – what a relief. Having ordered me to eat everything, he left. I wasn't hungry, but I managed to force most of it down. I toyed with the idea of leaving the rest, but, in the end, I stuffed that down too. Neil would have made me finish it anyway.

After a while he came back for the tray. Pulling back the bedclothes he examined me again, ordering me to turn over so he could inspect my back. He pronounced me unfit to play games that night and made me take some more tablets. As he disappeared to watch television, he told me he would be 'thinking up new games to play for when you have recovered'.

I went back to serenading myself in my head. It was strangely comforting. Mostly, I slept. During the night I woke up with a start, bathed in sweat. I was in agony with pains in my lower back, but mostly low down at the front, dull and then gripping pains. I had an urgent need to go to the toilet and it must be now. Without even waiting to ask, I slipped as quietly as I could out of bed and felt my way towards the bedroom door. The door was pushed to, but not shut. I eased it open, only as far as I needed to squeeze through; this I did hardly daring to breathe. I hadn't even noticed if Neil was in bed, although I presumed he was. I crept quietly into the bathroom, closed the door, put the light on and sank gratefully onto the loo. At the same time I was gripped by a pain so ferocious that I had to stuff my hand in my mouth to stop myself from crying out.

I wasn't sure what was happening. I'd had a wee, but I didn't feel any better. I still felt as though I needed a wee, and now I needed to move my bowels, but I couldn't. I was in a lot of pain and I'd been in there for ages. At first the pains were coming and going, now they were there most of the time. Every so often I was gripped by a really ferocious pain. I really felt like I wanted to move my bowels and I kept trying but I just couldn't.

When I came into the bathroom it was five o'clock. I knew because I had looked at Neil's watch, which he'd left on the bathroom sink. Now it was just after six. Stuff was starting to come away, like a really bad period, only worse, much worse. I didn't dare look. This was awful – it must have been a miscarriage, it must have been my baby, dying or dead. I didn't know what to do, I was so scared. I felt ill, shaking all over. What should I do?

Eventually it stopped. I knew I had to do something – Neil would be up and about at seven thirty. I did not want him to find out what had happened, not yet. I flushed the toilet and I kept flushing. I had a bath – how he didn't hear I don't know. I opened the bathroom window to let the steam out as I dried myself. I hid the wet towel under a pile of clean towels.

Oh shit, I'm stuffed! I thought to myself, as I looked down at the floor. It was splattered with blood, and so were my legs. Of course, after a baby, you bleed. Well, what could I do now? I screamed at myself, inside my head, as I grabbed another towel and stuffed it between my legs. I wiped blood from the floor with a flannel. Just then I heard his alarm go off. Bugger, bugger, bugger! Toilet, yes, I thought, throwing the flannel and the towel, which I whipped out from in-between my legs, into the bottom of the airing cupboard. Then I literally launched myself at the toilet. I was trying to get my breathing under control and wipe sweat from my face and between my breasts, when it registered somewhere in the back of my mind: that's the postman, must be early today; he doesn't normally come until after Neil has gone to work.

Meanwile I heard Neil get up, then his dangerously silky voice enquiring who had given me permission to either leave his bed or go to the toilet. He must have headed towards the front door to pick up the post.

'Sorry, sorry, Neil,' I shouted. 'I've got a really bad stomach. I've been in here for ages, I think it must have been that milk.' No reply. It was very quiet. The suspense was killing me, but I didn't dare get up off the toilet.

The bathroom door suddenly bounced off the wall with a bang as Neil came crashing through it. His face was screwed up and contorted with rage. He was waving something white in his hand. Lifting me off the toilet by my throat, he flung me into the hall where he stood over me as I lay cowering on the floor.

'Kill my baby. Kill my baby, would you? You fucking bitch. Well, I'm going to fucking kill you, and don't think for one moment it's going to be quick. I'm going to kill this fucking bitch as well.' At that point he waved the white thing in his hand in the air. 'When did you plan all this? What fucking pills? Where are they? Tell me now, if you want to spare your miserable friend's life.'

He grabbed me by the throat again, choking me and shaking me like a rag doll at the same time. 'Get up, stand up, stand up!' He was incandescent with rage as he dragged me to my feet by my throat. Grabbing me by my hair, he howled like a wild animal and headbutted me in the face. I was screaming with fear now. He had only once before hit me in a temper; the very first time. He was out of control. This noise was too much.

Someone was knocking on the door, then I heard Janet's voice asking if everything was all right. He put his fist up to my face as a warning to me to shut up. Instantly I became silent. I could see he was having a problem controlling himself. After a couple of minutes he shouted back we were fine, nothing to worry about, Janet, that he would call round and explain later.

After she had gone, he threw the letter down on the hall floor. 'I'm going to work now. I'm late already. This is your friend's reply to the letter you sent her, when you went behind your husband's back, asking for pills to kill – murder – his baby. I'll be back at six o'clock tonight. We will be having a full and frank discussion about this. Then you will be punished, do you understand?'

Somehow, through my swollen mouth and damaged teeth, I managed to get him to understand that I had already lost the baby. 'Spend the day grieving for yourself then, because your life is over.' He left me where he had dropped me, on the hall floor beside the letter from Chrissie. With shaking hands I picked it up. In the letter she said she couldn't help me and advised me to see a doctor as soon as possible.

About twenty or thirty minutes after Neil had gone to work, Janet came back round. I had managed to dress myself but couldn't hide my ruined face and she was absolutely horrified when she saw me. After what Neil had just said to me I knew I had to get out. It was either run, or sit and wait to die. I told Janet that Neil had gone berserk when he found out I'd lost the baby and that I was desperate to get away because he had threatened me, but I didn't have any money. Janet gave me some sanitary towels because I was still bleeding, and also told me that the welfare officer would provide me with money to get home. I'd never heard of them and had no idea where the office was – she had to tell me which bus to catch and where to get off, as well as giving me the bus fare.

I was in such a state that I walked out of the flat without my handbag or coat, closing the door behind me. It locked, and I didn't have a key (had never been allowed one). Even though it was January and freezing, I was too anxious to be gone to even try to get back inside. I left everything and just ran!

Chapter Twenty

THE WOMAN IN THE Welfare Office was not very cooperative. Nobody could say she was a pushover, that's for sure. I had tried to explain to her about the violence in the relationship and the miscarriage but without going into everything too deeply. First, because most of what happened in my relationship with Neil was beyond most people's understanding and belief. Secondly, I didn't want to be there all day; I wanted to be on my way as I didn't want Neil to catch up with me before I was home with Mum and Dad. I needed to be safe and I couldn't relax until I was.

She started by giving me the third degree about the miscarriage. How did I know I was actually pregnant when I hadn't seen a doctor? How did I know I had lost the baby? Why hadn't I kept what came away? Women normally kept what came away, saved it in a bucket and took it to the doctor. That's what she said. I felt really stupid; I didn't know how to answer any of these questions. Simple ignorance on my part relating to saving what came away and taking it to the doctor, I'm afraid, and fear. I was so afraid of what Neil would do to me once he realized I had lost the baby; I just wanted to get rid of the evidence as soon as possible. What she was saying, in effect, was that I was accusing my husband of beating me up and causing a miscarriage when I had no proof I was even pregnant.

Then she turned her attention to the violence in the relationship. She looked at my face. By this time, my two front teeth were kind of at an angle, pushed backwards. My mouth was swollen and red, as were my nose and eyes. My neck was not yet bruised, but was also red and swollen and thumbprints could clearly be seen where Neil had tried to strangle me. With a straight face she asked me to consider the possibility that I may be exaggerating the seriousness of the attack; that perhaps I was making a mountain out of a molehill. Maybe I should wait until Neil came home, try to sit down and calmly and rationally sort things out.

After the way I had been forced to live over the past year, it was really hard for me to stand up for myself. I still don't know how I managed it but my fear and desperation must have given me strength. Somehow I came out of that office with enough money or perhaps a travel warrant (I can't actually remember). This woman prevaricated so much about the inconvenience I was causing, I thought I would explode with tension. I crept out of that office feeling like the lowest of the low, especially after the way she looked down her nose at me, which reinforced my already low opinion of myself. All the time she was asking me questions, I was thinking: you have no idea what I have been through, what I have had to endure, what I have just survived; don't belittle me and hammer me into the ground like this; I wouldn't wish what I have experienced on anybody, have some compassion, it's not even your money I'm asking for.

I don't remember too much about the journey itself, only how cold I felt. I was absolutely freezing and shaking, not just from the cold but also from shock. I was a young and attractive young woman and I was used to being stared at and wolf-whistled at by men. But I wasn't used to being an object of curiosity and ridicule. Everywhere I went that day people stared at me, nudged each other, pointed, tutted, looked at each other knowingly. At a main-line railway station I had to wait half an hour for a connection. I went to the toilet where a young Irish woman trapped me in a corner. She was obviously having a bad trip on something, probably LSD; she was shouting and screaming obscenities at me, waving her arms about.

'I was once beautiful like you, look at me now,' she

yelled. 'This is a warning, you stupid fucking cow. If you don't want to end up looking like me, stay off the fucking drugs. People used to bloody well look at me the fucking way they're staring at you. But not any fucking more they don't.' On and on she went. Every time I tried to get away, she would push me back into the corner. She was totally off her trolley. Eventually, I ducked under her arm when she was distracted by somebody else shouting at her to shut up. In the fragile condition I was in at the time I found her very unnerving.

There was no heating at all on the train and I hugged myself, unable to stop shivering. There were six gentlemen of foreign nationality in my carriage who spent most of the journey staring, pointing and nodding at me. They were obviously talking about me. I wanted them to ask me if I was okay but then again, any human kindness might have brought my fragile 'house of cards' crashing down. I needed to stay strong. I was like a homing pigeon – I had to get to Mum and Dad's, then I could fall to pieces.

After the train journey, I had a taxi ride of about ten miles. At least the taxi had heating but unfortunately I was so cold by this time that the journey wasn't long enough for me to warm myself up before I got home. I arrived in the early hours of the morning and I had to knock my family up out of bed.

It was my nana who came downstairs and let me in. She took me into the kitchen, turned on the one-bar gas fire and gave me a long, pink candlewick dressing gown to put on over my clothes. I was still freezing cold and couldn't stop shaking. Nana filled the kettle with water, switched it on and gave me a warm, loving cuddle. Her eyes filled up with tears and she just kept saying, 'Eh lass, eh lass, it's good to have you back safe at home. You'll be all right now lass, you'll see.' My dam broke and the tears came. I put my arms around her and we wept together as the kettle came to the boil.

Mum was at last alerted to the fact that something was afoot in the house and appeared in the kitchen. When she saw the state of me she was very upset, but by this time Nana, who was buttering toast, was on a roll. 'I said no good would come of sending her back there with him. Just look at the state of the lass. Look at the state of her. Nobody should have to put up with that kind of treatment. I don't care what they've done – and she's done nowt. I don't care what Neil says. She's done nowt to deserve that – he should be "castarated" he should. That's what should happen to him, he should be "castarated". I don't know what her father was thinking about, sending her back there with him.'

Mum reached out for my hand. 'All right Mother,

she's upset enough without you starting. Let her get this tea and toast, she's absolutely freezing cold.'

It was very difficult for me to eat – my mouth was sore and my teeth were a problem. While I struggled, Mum had a couple of cigarettes and we all drank lots of tea, which was easier for me to manage with a straw. Painfully, both emotionally and physically (because talking hurt my mouth), I told them about the miscarriage. They were both sympathetic but said it was probably for the best. Perhaps it had happened because there was something wrong with the baby. I hadn't managed to tell them yet that Neil beat me up when we got home after the last weekend with them. Mum had made the assumption that the cause of the miscarriage came originally from the beating Neil had given me when she was staying at the flat, believing that this must have damaged the baby in some way. She was probably right and I didn't want them to feel worse than they needed to for sending me back.

I also explained about the letter I had written to Chrissie, and how Neil had read it. I had expected them to be shocked that I wanted to end my pregnancy and they were. Although they could see why I was worried Neil might hurt the baby, because I couldn't bring myself to tell them everything Neil had done to me they didn't really understand how I could have been desperate enough to believe that ending my pregnancy was the right thing to do. My nana had suffered a lot of miscarriages and my mother was a surviving twin so I could also see their point of view. They both said it was a relief to them that the decision had been taken out of my hands through the the miscarriage.

Nana had put hot water bottles in my bed and, tucked up under the covers, I was beginning to feel warm at last. I was so tired and it was good to feel safe. As I was drifting into sleep I thought about my nana, and how her Lancashire accent and the dialect always came out most strongly when she was upset; also, how she never missed an opportunity to have a go at Dad and put him down, as in, 'I don't know what her father was thinking about, sending her back there.' Then my thoughts floated on to Mum, and how she left everything practical to everyone else. She hadn't appeared downstairs until after the tea and toast were made and the fire on. No filling of hot water bottles for my mum, Nana did that too. I was really glad to be back, but nothing had changed. This was still my original prison.

I didn't see my dad until after he got back from work the following day. Typically we never really talked about what happened. My dad wasn't one for talking about his feelings. He never, ever admitted when he was in the wrong and never said sorry to anybody about anything, even when he was. Still, without saying anything to me, I know he never forgave himself for sending me back with Neil that day. My mum and dad, they aren't perfect, they've made a lot of mistakes, but one thing I do know about them is that they do really love me.

Mum had sent for Doctor Butcher first thing the next morning. He had been our family doctor since before I was born. She made me move bedrooms and get into her bed, the way she did when I was a child with chickenpox, waiting for Dr Butcher to come and make me feel better. He called around sometime in the afternoon. I heard Mum whispering to him downstairs, then he came bustling into the bedroom all cheerful and friendly. 'Your mum tells me you've been having a bit of a difficult time lately, young lady. How are you feeling today?'

'Not too bad thanks, Doctor.' I struggled to sit up and speak in a coherent way through the disaster area I now called my mouth.

'There's a distinct possibility you've had a miscarriage I believe. Just let me have a feel of your tummy.'

My face must have gone as white as chalk as I clutched the bedclothes to my breasts. 'It's all right, not to panic; I'll just have a feel through your nightie, no problem, there we go.' He pulled back the bedclothes and made various doctor noises. 'Well, I don't think there's much doubt there, you probably were pregnant, but sadly not anymore. Let's leave things as they are at the moment. If the bleeding doesn't settle down, any problems with your next period, pop in and see me, okay?'

He wasn't too impressed with the state of my face and advised me to see a dentist sooner rather than later. The other bruising and swelling was, he said, superficial and would heal itself fairly quickly. He enquired how it had happened and, before I could reply, Mum told him my husband had headbutted me. Whereupon Doctor Butcher looked me straight in the eyes (he had kind twinkly blue eyes) and laughingly asked, 'Well, you're a big girl now, why didn't you hit him back?'

The room began to spin. I felt like I was disappearing down a deep, dark hole into nothingness. I was nothing, I am nothing. I had escaped from nothing. This was not freedom.

As my healing process began, so did my descent into madness.

Chapter Twenty-One

A S THE DOCTOR LEFT the room, leaving me feeling dazed and numb, I became fully aware of my surroundings – the patterned wallpaper, the furniture, the familiar clean smell of the bedroom – and the feeling of being safe began to change into a black reality. While I was grateful to have a safe place to live, it was hard to find myself slipping into the old soul-destroying patterns: acting as unpaid babysitter to my brothers, becoming cleaner, cook and parent figure to my own mother, and peacemaker between my nana and Dad. My dreams of escaping from this family situation, the small-town rural oblivion, to a happy future had turned out to be a fifteen-month-long nightmare. I was back where the story began; only now the essence of my life lay seriously fragmented around me.

Oddly enough the one thing that terrified me the most – that Neil would come to get me and I would find myself back in hell — never happened. I couldn't believe that he would let me go that easily and for a long time I would try to second-guess what he would do. Would I receive a letter apologizing for his behaviour, swearing undying love? Perhaps there would be a knock at the door one day, and there he would be, appearing contrite. 'I don't know what got into me,' he would say. 'Please come back.' Maybe the real Neil would arrive one dark night as I was walking home. The connotations of that were too horrific for my mind to take the scenario any further.

I don't know why he didn't contact me. Perhaps once I had escaped he knew he would not be able to regain control over me, and that this time my parents would not be so easily persuaded that the fault lay with me. He divorced me a few years later — our solicitors handled it and I didn't have to set eyes on him.

Although I had escaped Neil, I could never escape the damage he had perpetrated. It was insidious, seeping into and contaminating every area of my life — my beliefs, thoughts, feelings, actions and reactions. Everything that happened from now on was to have a direct or indirect connection with that damage.

My ability to evaluate everything in life was distorted. I was grieving the loss of a baby, but also carrying the guilt of not wanting Neil's child. It is very difficult to give any adequate description of how Neil had severed the main emotional arteries that had once energized a bubbly teenage girl. I could no longer distinguish between love and fear. He had amputated the key elements of my self-expression. Through his violence, he had injected me with an addiction to adrenalin. His sexual abuse, used to degrade and humiliate me, to satisfy him and give him a sense of power, had destroyed any link between love and sex. I began to despise all men. I was completely isolated again, my mind in turmoil, with no one to help me. The door had slammed shut, trapping me inside the prison of my wounded mind.

Looking at the crumbled state of my life I wondered how I could turn the clock back, to return to normality. How could I erase the last dreadful fifteen months and pick up the pieces? In an endeavour to do this I contacted Andrew, my last boyfriend before Neil. After my experiences over the last few months, life with him now seemed almost like heaven; I remembered feeling safe, secure and cared for then.

Hoping against hope, I called Andrew, told him I had had a miscarriage and hinted that the relationship with Neil had been violent. He was not sympathetic or interested, and made it quite clear he was getting his life back together and that he was in a new relationship. As we talked he became angry, saying that I had really hurt him and he wasn't prepared to allow himself to be vulnerable again. He was right, of course, and I was just being very selfish, but I was also feeling desperately unhappy and lonely. It would never have worked though; my head was far too mixed up and I was clutching at straws. I somehow had to summon up the courage to make a new start.

In my endeavours to give a description of my life and thinking from this point on, I am finding myself confronted with quite a difficult analysis. In retrospect, it is very easy to see the events that affected the early part of my life, and it would be very nice to be able to set out defined incidents where I put my life back on track. But mine has been a slow, complicated, 'one step forward, two steps back' recovery.

On the surface I appeared to be a happy-go-lucky, bubbly flirt – a young woman out for a good time, with no strings attached. Scratch the surface and just underneath was my anger towards Neil, now projected onto all men, along with my grief over the miscarriage and my relationship, mixed with the guilt I felt for wanting to abort the foetus.

At the time I believed I needed a man to make me happy and fulfilled, and that I couldn't survive without one. I also believed that I didn't have much going for me, apart from my looks. I never forgot the phrase my dad used when I failed my 11-plus, that it was lucky I was so attractive. As he said, 'there's nothing worse than being thick *and* ugly'. Being pretty and outgoing, I was able to obtain work in a cocktail bar during the day and early evening, and a disco late at night. In this environment, I observed what occurred in the nightlife of that small town. The number of seemingly happily married men that were out on the pull reinforced my low opinion of the trustworthiness of men. It was very easy to fall into this infectious shallow lifestyle, in which, ironically, I was able to satisfy my addiction to adrenalin and danger by having numerous clandestine affairs with an abundance of suitable targets. I was under the misapprehension that to have sex with these men and then dump them was satisfying my need for revenge.

Within a few months there was a cold, brief blast from the past. One of my colleagues, an attractive married girl called Sadie, was having the odd fling with some of the men who frequented the bar. One night her husband came into the bar to give her a message, believing she would be there working. He was shocked when he discovered that she wasn't there, and went to look for her. The following day, the town was swarming with policemen. She had been found dead, and her husband had committed suicide.

This incident affected me greatly, reminding me of

the violence I had suffered and making me wonder if I had really escaped from Neil. It also made me very nervous about having an affair that might put me in a dangerous situation. Subsequently I began to search again for the ideal man, and I briefly thought I'd found one in Sam. When I became pregnant I was absolutely ecstatic – never had a baby been so wanted or so loved. Sam promised he would stand by me and that we would make a family life together, and in my confusion I persuaded myself that I loved him and things would be all right. Really, I had just wanted a sperm donor.

I was still living with my parents at the time and their reaction to my news was not joyful, or even positive. Here was a secret that couldn't be kept quiet – already I was beginning to show. Finally the town gossips would be right: shamefully, in their eyes, I was single and pregnant.

'What are the neighbours going to say?' my mother huffed as my dad shook his head in disgust and asked when I was going to be moving out.

Sam smoothed things over by talking about how he was going to be looking for a flat for us in his home town. But he never did find us anywhere to live and after my beautiful daughter Katrina was born I began to feel that his commitment was not strong enough for either her or me. For my child's sake I found the strength to terminate our relationship, although I left the door open for him to have a relationship with her. My intuition about him was correct, because he declined to take any responsibility towards her upbringing. I didn't care though: I was totally engrossed with my new, happy little baby.

Although I continued to work in a bar in the evenings, I did not go out with anyone for the next few months until one night I met a man who was an engineer. We had a relationship for about four months before we moved into a flat together. I had thought long and hard before moving in with him – it was a big step for me, given what had happened the last time I lived with a man and my head was in conflict, thoughts spinning round. But I had begun to feel that I needed a man, and that my daughter needed a father, and I believed we would all live happily ever after.

We had two blissful months together before he told me he was married with two children and was still living with his wife. Suddenly, everything fell into place: the many meetings he had to attend, the weekends away when he was catching up on his business. I had given him my trust and now I was totally devastated. How could I have been so stupid? I should have known better; you can't trust men. What made it worse, he blatantly expected to continue the polygamous relationship with me, and still remain married to his wife. I had just been the 'bit on the side'. It reinforced what my mum always used to say: 'Men only want you for one thing, and once they've got it, they're not interested any more.'

Following my pattern, I had six months away from men, licking my wounds, then, rather like a drug addict craving the next fix of adrenalin, I drifted back into casual relationships, this time with colourful characters.

I was still confused when my second husband, Ken, came on the scene. I had known him for some time and liked him because he had a wicked sense of humour and always made me laugh. He was about ten years older than me and owned his own business, which he had inherited from his father. An only child, he was a bit of a mummy's boy and liked his own way but he was also solid and dependable, the kind of man you knew you could take home to meet your parents and they would approve of him. He got on well with Katrina, and she loved him.

After about six months we got married, and because we were good friends we were happy together. This situation changed when his former wife remarried and her new husband wanted to adopt Ken's son.

Although he agreed to this, Ken could not really cope with the reality of it, and he began to take his frustration out on Katrina. She suffered greatly with his mood

swings, and when I saw Ken throw her across the floor
one day and tell her that he hated her, I knew we
couldn't continue this way. I told him that for my
daughter's sake it would be better if we parted. He
wanted us to stay together and was very upset, although
not prepared to change his attitude towards her. He knew
he was being unreasonable but just could not cope with
his feelings.

Our separation was very bitter and he stopped paying
any bills relating to our home. I had no knowledge of
this until one dreadful day when the news of repossession,
and gas and electricity being disconnected arrived in the
same post. I was now in complete panic. I had nowhere
to turn for help, with no access to the kind of money
needed to pay off the debts and enable me to keep a roof
over Katrina's head, much less provide her with a stable
home. Looking back over her young life and the
decisions I had made, all of them bad ones, I realized I
was a failure as a mother. It's as though I shone a spotlight
on myself and at last saw clearly the mess I had made.

I fell into a deep dark hole that I could not climb out
of. All reason must have left me because I decided to trust
my beautiful daughter, the most precious thing in the
world to me, to the care of my own parents. Katrina was
safe at my parents' house and, in the minutes it took me

to take that decision, I believed that my mother, imperfect as she was, would do a much better job of looking after her than I could.

Then I took an overdose of pills.

Chapter Twenty-Two

I WAS FOUND BY A neighbour and rushed to hospital where they pumped my stomach and stabilized me. My depression was so severe I had to be taken into the local psychiatric hospital for two or three months, where I received electroconvulsive therapy.

I can remember very little about this period. For a long time after receiving ECT there were days when I could not recall my name, and I could not recognize people I knew. Even the clothes in my wardrobe seemed unrecognizable to me. Ironically, I never forgot the secrets of what had happened in my relationship with Neil.

About two weeks after I was discharged from the psychiatric hospital I tried to commit suicide again. As before, Katrina was with my parents and this time I took a lot more pills. I should have died; but again I was saved by pure chance when a friend called round to see me.

For three days I was in intensive care in a coma. As I slowly recovered, it dawned on me that perhaps I wasn't meant to die; that perhaps my little daughter and I deserved better. So I began to reassess my life; should I value myself more? From somewhere within I found a determination to change.

My first step was to apply to a secretarial college to take a training course. This was a big move forward in my healing process. To enable myself to have an income when Ken and I divorced, I had gone into modelling and promotions work. I had been using my external appearance to survive. By taking up this course I was beginning to acknowledge that I actually also had a brain.

Although I was excited to be studying again, it was not always easy to stay positive as I was being evicted from my home, and my only income was from the little bits of bar work or modelling that I could get. I was signed up to a modelling agency and around my twenty-sixth birthday they asked me to attend a photographic studio for a session. The job, should I be successful, was to do modelling and promotion work for a newspaper. I was in the studio waiting for the photographer to set up the shot, when into my life came the smell of expensive aftershave; in front of me stood a beautifully dressed, exquisitely groomed, well-spoken, confident man called Connor. He worked in management for the newspaper and had called round to discuss what the job entailed. We had a long conversation about what would be expected of me and as he spoke the tone of respect in his voice entered my head and heart, and made me feel human, a special person. I thought he was unobtainable, and was pleasantly surprised when he wanted to get to know me. The genuineness of the way he reached out to me triggered my intuition that this was the person I had been searching for.

Needless to say I did get the job.

There was something quite surreal about this meeting. Although I felt we both had a physical attraction towards each other, there was a much deeper connection too and over the next few weeks a close relationship developed. At first Connor politely rejected my advances, but in a nice way, and this endorsed my feeling that there was something very special between us. He was locked in an unhappy relationship and had a young son and at first his being married made me feel quite safe. Having recently gone through a bitter separation myself, I was more than a little shaky about getting too involved. Unfortunately, I very quickly fell deeply in love. This was not in the game plan. It was not good at all; I felt extremely vulnerable. To make matters worse, Katrina was equally besotted with him.

After a year at the Secretarial College for Young

Ladies I was extremely proud to finish the course with an impressive array of certificates in shorthand, typing and book-keeping. Having failed to complete my earlier education, it meant a lot to me that I had succeeded at this. When I quite easily got a job as a legal secretary, even my father was cautiously optimistic that I wasn't a complete waste of space. My mother, on the other hand, made a derisory comment about having the doorways made bigger to accommodate my head. For once I didn't let either of their reactions affect me. I was beginning to pay my way and value myself more.

After I'd been evicted, the local council had temporarily put me in a dilapidated old house, but my circumstances gave me priority on the housing list. Things were beginning to move for me, but although Connor and I were enjoying a very romantic, loving affair, nothing in my lover signalled that he wanted to make it more permanent. He was still living in the same house as his wife. His friends made me feel that I was just his latest dolly bird, arm candy. They said he'd had numerous affairs, that he was just a charmer, and that he wanted to leave his wife but never would because of his young son.

To me, at the time, there was some incongruity about the relationship. I knew he was very much in love with me and I felt the same but would it come to anything? I was so scared that if we continued to fall more deeply in love and then split up, I would not survive it. So I gave him an ultimatum: by the time the council had rehoused me, he had to have sorted out his other life. I felt he was being unfair to his wife and son, and I didn't want a part-time relationship either. Connor needed to decide whether he was staying with his wife and child, or leaving them. I wasn't insisting he came to live with me if he wasn't ready for that, but I needed him to show some commitment to our relationship. He was quite shocked, and although he did try to reassure me that we would be together eventually, he appeared not to react otherwise. All the old doubts began to raise their ugly heads again. I had been let down so many times before. Could I trust any man?

I was heartbroken, but hid behind my armour and, reverting back to type, I had an affair with the most unsuitable man I could find. I had to punish Connor – but who was I really punishing? I guess we all suffered in the end.

Mr Unsuitable quickly moved into my new home, which I had just been given by the council. He was very good at spending my money and emotionally it was a very traumatic relationship, both for Katrina and for me. Eventually, matters came to a head when he told me he had been having an affair with a girl who was not very pretty, but whose parents were loaded. He was going to get engaged but it was 'just business'. He twisted the knife even further by commenting that I was really good in bed, but definitely not marriage material, and it was time for him to move on. When I told him to go, he was actually quite shocked because for him it wasn't convenient to move out yet.

Occasionally I would go out with Connor. I still felt the same about him, and I knew he still felt the same about me, although we never told each other. In a way we didn't have to, but at the same time he was still with his wife. It used to light up my day when I saw him, but break my heart when I left him.

After Mr Unsuitable left, I dropped back into the brief affairs, the 'one-night stand syndrome' again. Then I went for the biggest letch and liar in town, a man who had fathered numerous children, and did not financially support any of them. I think in a strange way I saw him as a challenge. He moved into my house with his belongings a little bit at a time. I went out with him for about two or three months, until he went to work abroad on a three-month contract. He seemed to make his living this way; away for three months, home for a couple of months. I didn't go out whilst he was abroad, and when he came back, he had bought me an engagement ring. He proposed and I said yes, although even at the time I didn't really believe we would actually get married. Strangely for a newly engaged man, for the rest of his leave he barely spent any time with me. I thought he was catching up with his mates but still, it puzzled me greatly that, instead of growing, his curly hair was getting shorter and shorter by the day. Then I heard he was having an affair. I challenged him but he denied it strenuously. I was particularly worried because by now my period was two weeks late. When I mentioned this to him, he went crazy.

He became violent, and threw me from one end of the hall to the other. I hit my head badly on the back door, and was knocked out and concussed. When I came round I was alone on the floor. I felt very frightened and depressed. I had been here before – different hall, different floor, but the same place. Two days later Mr Unsuitable turned up, all apologetic, and persuaded me to give him another chance. He was due to go off abroad again and insisted on taking me out to dinner before he went. That night in the restaurant, whilst he was in the toilets, the owner (who was a good friend of mine) told me to be careful. It turned out that Mr Unsuitable had just recently become engaged to a ladies' hairdresser, a neighbour of mine. That's why the curly hair didn't bloody grow! It was classic; he had made a fool of me. When he left my house I told him to take everything that was his with him. It was over between us and any belongings he left would go straight in the rubbish bin.

Reflecting on the incident in the hall, and the fact that my period started shortly after the bump on my head, I had a strong feeling of déjà vu. My life had gone full circle. Although feeling low, I began to reassess everything yet again, and made up my mind that the way forward was not to go out and jump into bed with the first man that came along. That was the last thing I wanted. I had started to value myself at last. I knew I deserved better than that.

A few weeks after the departure of the multi-engaged, short-haired bastard, there was a knock at my door. I immediately recognized the expensive aftershave. In front of me was Connor, clutching a large bunch of roses and smiling. He had come to invite me to dinner. I hadn't seen him for months as he had been away a lot on trips abroad as an international sales manager for a local company, but the instant I laid eyes on him the old feelings came flooding back. Over dinner he told me he had finally made the break from his wife, and had been offered a job in South Africa. He had accepted and wanted to catch up with me before he went – he hoped we would stay in touch.

If, like me, you believe in synchronicity, you will not

be surprised by his reappearance. After our dinner date, he stayed the night. Needless to say, he never caught that plane to Cape Town. And twenty-six years down the line we are still very much in love, although life has not always been easy.

Chapter Twenty-Three

OPENING THE DOOR TO Connor that day, it seemed that my adolescent dreams had finally come true; my knight in shining armour had arrived to set my world to rights. Although this is fairy-tale, magical thinking, it is true that a light came into both of our lives.

We had been together only a few months, blissfully happy, and even had a new member of the family, an old English sheepdog, when my dad was diagnosed with a terminal illness. As well as being a great shock, it was very stressful and emotionally draining for the whole family. Connor and I tried hard to make the time he had left as enjoyable as possible. We took Mum and Dad out whenever we could, and despite the tragedy of it all, it was lovely to see them enjoy and rekindle the warmth and closeness of their earlier loving relationship.

Dad's health soon began to deteriorate and he did not wish to go into hospital. He became confined to bed, needing twenty-four-hour care, and I gave up my job to look after him. For the last few weeks of his life my mum couldn't cope, either emotionally or physically, with helping to look after him. This isn't uncommon in these situations; it did, however, make it much harder for me. It was also Mum's way of dealing with things, by literally not dealing with them. It was hard for her to be grown up. Two days before Dad died, he was taken into hospital, but by then he was unaware of what was going on around him.

Katrina struggled to cope with her granddad's illness. He had been her father substitute; they were very close and adored each other. He was a proud, strong-willed man who wanted his granddaughter to remember him as fit and healthy and so he would not allow her into the bedroom, no matter how desperate she was to see him. She was very confused and wanted to know what she had done to upset him. Bearing in mind the abandonment by her biological father, after Dad died she was left with the feeling that everyone she loved would leave her, and that it must somehow be her own fault.

When Dad died, I was relieved at first that his suffering was over. It wasn't until I saw the coffin in the church that the loss really hit me. I sobbed all through the funeral service, on the way to the cemetery, during the burial and until halfway through the funeral tea. I remember telling someone off for laughing. I couldn't understand why people were enjoying themselves, eating and knocking back the drink, although it was what Dad would have wanted.

Afterwards I felt as though a huge weight had been lifted off my shoulders. He wasn't there to disapprove of me any more and I could let go of the guilt of having let him down. I sometimes wondered how he would feel now. Would he have been proud of what I have achieved? At the end of the day, it's not actually important any more, because what I have done, I have done for me, and not for him.

Connor had left his job even though it was extremely well paid and he really enjoyed it. It had suited his lifestyle perfectly before we got together, but now he hated being away from me, especially when I was trying to cope with Dad's illness. Instead he had taken a number of 'tide me over', lower-paid jobs. Not the best money manager, he was struggling to keep up maintenance payments to his ex-wife and we went through a difficult time financially.

He began to look for a better job and out of the blue was offered a high-profile post in the Middle East. He got the phone call offering him the job on a Wednesday and had to fly out on the Friday. It would be about five weeks before Katrina and I could join him. In that traditional community it was not really acceptable for us to be living together so a couple of months after we arrived, we got married. It wasn't the usual wedding – just a civil ceremony followed by a good party. Quite a lot of people turned up and it was a multicultural celebration. A wealthy Sheikh appeared and was followed within minutes by a crate of expensive champagne. Neither Connor nor I had ever seen him before, and we went over to thank him. We asked what his name was, and he answered 'Issa', which I believe is Arabic for Jesus. We spent the next two days in a top hotel where Katrina told everyone we were all on our honeymoon. I think she enjoyed it more than we had the chance to!

I took a job as personal assistant to the vice president of a well-known offshore bank and our life settled into a routine. At first it was like a grand holiday; swimming everyday, many cocktail parties, a good social life, and a nanny provided. Being many miles from home brought us all closer together. However, our twelve months there showed us what an unfair place the world is, as we witnessed both extreme poverty and vast wealth and abuse of power. There was quite a bit of political unrest and instability in that part of the world and because Connor worked in the media he was a target. After a couple of incidents, it was thought best if a few of the staff returned to Britain till things blew over. Connor was one of those picked to leave, and as I was now pregnant I was quite relieved. We'd had good and bad times in the Middle East but towards the end it was quite frightening.

We settled happily back in Britain, with the exciting prospect of a new addition to the family to look forward to. I remembered so well the much longed-for and joyous arrival of my baby girl. She was an easy child, sleeping through the night, always happy and contented, with a smile for everyone. Expecting history to repeat itself, I was surprised to see that I had just given birth to a beautiful baby boy with hair like a lavatory brush but with quite a different temper. Right from the start it was clear that Jack had a determined personality and he wasn't going to just fit in with anyone. His attitude was, and still is, 'Here I am, this is me. If you've got a problem, it's your problem. Deal with it!' Yes, the whole family was in no doubt; a star was born.

Connor really loves kids and had this naïve fantasy that a house full of children would be such a fun place to be. Having just about got used to coping with our demanding little son, I became pregnant again. Unfortunately, after about four months I had a miscarriage, followed by all the usual emotions and sadness. Still being the adoring wife, going along with Connor's fantasy, and this time enjoying my relatively new motherhood, I became pregnant again.

Our second lovely daughter, Mikaela, was born two months premature with a heart condition and had to be kept in hospital for six weeks. For almost a full year she cried constantly and there was nothing we could do to make it better. When she almost died and was rushed back into hospital the powers that be decided to send her to see a top heart consultant who realized that she had a heart problem. She was immediately transferred to a specialist heart hospital, one of the saddest places I have ever been. All the children were very ill and every day I would see young children going for serious operations. Their parents were distraught and I felt their silent prayers and shared their fears and hopes, if only as a witness.

Mikaela had to have two heart operations and they were possibly the worst moments of my life. I carried her on the short walk to the operating theatre for her second operation and as we got near she recognized the smell, and saw the nurses and surgeons in their green gowns and masks. Her little frail arms clung to me and drained me of every resource I had. I could hardly bear to let a nurse take her from me.

In my utter desperation I felt totally inadequate. Like all parents in this situation, I silently cried out to the emptiness and wished I could swap places with her. I searched hard for God and, in all this turmoil, I feel I had a spiritual experience. I was praying and bargaining that, if my little baby could come through this operation, I would sort myself out and somehow use my life's experiences to help others. I had come a long way in piecing back together the jigsaw of my shattered mind and emotions. I was a lot better, but acknowledged I needed to go much further.

As the hours passed, I lost track of time. I went into a trance-like state and subconsciously fought alongside my brave little fighter for her life. I was in a daze when the ward doors opened and this frail little being was wheeled in. Tubes seemed to emerge from all angles of her tiny body. Somehow I knew that now she would be all right. Connor was looking after the other two children and arrived a couple of hours after the operation. Uneasy with all the drips and drains, Mikaela lay there, still drowsy from the anaesthetic. When she heard her father's voice, she gave him a smile he says he will never forget.

What was this strange spiritual experience? In times of crisis I had cried out for help so many times before. Each of us has our own personal religious beliefs. I feel on that day, as the theatre doors closed behind Mikaela, a life more precious to me than my own, on a higher level somewhere she opened another door for me. Help and guidance came from somewhere. Was I beginning to recognize and have communion with my higher self?

Remembering other times in my life when I had felt

very low, I realized that somehow I had always found the inner strength to keep going. Eventually, my life would slightly change direction, giving me new strength and hope to continue to learn and grow. Even my two serious attempts at suicide hadn't been successful. I began to accept that perhaps something was watching over me and guiding me. That is when I started to understand how we needed to heal the whole person – mentally, emotionally and spiritually. Of course, at this stage in my life it was no more than a vague notion. It wasn't until two or three years later, when I was having therapy myself and training to be a hypnotherapist, that I really understood what it meant.

Connor and I are both very complex individuals, and we have both struggled with problems from our pasts. We certainly, especially in the early years of our relationship, had trauma and anxiety, and supported each other as best we could. As my confidence grew, I became more aware that I needed to work through the problems stemming from my childhood and this I did with the help of a hypnotherapist. That's how I also found a new direction in my life. Knowing how much the therapy had helped me, I very much wanted to dedicate myself to enabling others to heal their inner wounded child.

Encouraged and supported by Connor, I took up my education again when the children were still young. We shared the chores, and would often work into the early hours of the morning, discussing my homework long after the children were tucked up in bed. In what seems like a relatively short time now, I passed my GCSEs and three A-levels, and trained as a curative hypnotherapist. I gained diplomas in counselling and other areas related to my work, including a Teacher's Training Certificate. While all this was happening, I opened my own private practice in 1987, and began teaching workshops and night classes at an adult education centre, eventually becoming involved in training students to become counsellors. I am still a practising counsellor and curative hypnotherapist.

Connor and I are soul mates in the real sense of the words; we are still very much in love. It has been a long time since we met in that photographer's studio, but I feel that in the intervening years, none of which have been easy, we have both learned the meaning of true intimacy in an adult relationship.

Katrina, my first very special daughter, was often a guiding light when hope was gone, and over the years she and Connor have built a very loving relationship. Then Jack and Mikaela came along, and all three in their own unique ways have made their contribution towards enriching our lives tremendously. Blessed with their unconditional love, I have found the strength to write this book.

I think the flashbacks that set me on this journey arrived at a point in my life when I was finally ready to deal with my most painful and deeply hidden secrets. Before Neil and I were married, I loved to sing and dance. Forty years on, I am only just beginning to sing again. I still can't bring myself to dance yet. But one day I will.

Conclusion

M Y STORY IS NOT UNIQUE, as abusive relationships tend to follow a certain pattern. If you have suffered from domestic violence you may find echoes of your own experiences in these pages.

As you are reading this book you are probably aware what a widespread issue domestic violence actually is. However, even those of us who are aware do not fully appreciate the magnitude of the problem and the lack of adequate resources to cope with it, until we look at some of the facts and figures.

For example, *every minute* in the United Kingdom the police receive a phone call for assistance in relation to a case of domestic violence. However, according to the British Crime Survey (2003–4) only 40.2 per cent of actual domestic violence is ever reported to the police. In 2003–4 there were 276 refuges in England, helping over 18,000 women and 23,084 children, but this figure is not the full picture. How many complaints are not getting through to the police and how many victims are not getting the help they so urgently need?

I hope this book will increase public awareness and concern over the issue and will enable survivors of domestic violence to come to terms with and make sense of their experiences within their relationships. I am living proof that healing works, that if you look at the issues that have arisen in your childhood and overcome them, you can stop the cycle of domestic violence and increase your self-esteem and confidence.

I hope this book will also help the staff of the appropriate agencies and the refuges – who are already doing an excellent job, often under extremely stressful and difficult circumstances – to have a better understanding when dealing with vulnerable people like me, and that, knowing where we are coming from, they will be more aware of the issues involved. This will enable them to offer the right help and support to domestic abuse survivors to rebuild their lives constructively. If you have never experienced violence in your life, this book may give you some insights into what it feels like to be a victim.

Here I would like to put my counsellor's hat on and give a very brief and basic explanation of how children like me, who grew up in a dysfunctional family, end up with a distorted belief system that is taken into our adult lives; and why we, in our adult relationships, are targets for abusers.

I must stress that this is a very simple analysis and I have done my best to write it in terms which everyone can understand, steering away as much as possible from 'counsellor speak'.

So let us begin the analysis . . .

The Inner Belief System

Each of us has our own unique map of the world we live in; it is called our inner belief system. All our beliefs about ourselves and the world, how we feel the world relates to us, and how we in turn relate to the world are stored in our subconscious minds. Also stored there are our earliest feelings and memories, which were formed around what was happening in our childhood and the conditions in which we lived.

As children, if we are brought up believing that our parents' love, and the love of other adults who have influence over us, is conditional – i.e. given only *if* we are good, *if* we are well behaved, *if* we get it right – then as adults we will still believe we are only lovable if we meet these same conditions. That is, we will not feel worthy of being loved and accepted for just who we are.

Each child growing up will be confronted with events that we call 'crisis times'. These are like signposts to life. At these times we can grow or deteriorate. The responses that people give us at these crisis times will in all probability form the basis for our reactions later in life because we will have accepted these responses as the truth. It was only in writing this book that a bit of my own emotional jigsaw fell into place. Recalling the awful time when my baby brother Joe was badly scalded, and the way my mother told me God would strike me down, I realized that subconsciously I believed that I deserved to be punished.

In an idealistic situation, children who do experience unconditional love, regardless of their faults, shortcomings or mistakes, will survive, be more positive and more likely to realize their full potential. (This is not to say that parents should encourage their child to believe they are perfect even when they are behaving badly. One should always make a distinction between the child and its behaviour: 'I love you unconditionally but that behaviour is unacceptable.')

From the moment we are born we need to believe that our parents are like God: they know everything. If anything goes wrong, either in our relationship with our parents or their relationship with each other, as young children we blame ourselves. It's easier for us to accept we are unlovable than that our parents are not perfect.

Because, if our parents are not perfect, how can they take care of our every need, and so the world outside is an even more frightening place to be. Children think ego-centrically, they personalize everything. If Dad has no time for me, that means something's wrong with me. This is how children interpret abuse: 'It must be my fault.' When our needs as children are not met, our adult life is contaminated by our inner child's way of thinking.

The belief system I brought with me from early childhood was:

I am unlovable.

I cannot trust myself, my feelings, my intuition.

I am a failure.

I am a powerless victim.

This bad thing is only happening to me because although I may look okay on the outside, inside I am ugly.

If something is wrong, it's my fault and I have to try harder to get it right.

How Our Inner Belief System Relates to the Inner Child

In counselling terms we all have what is known as the 'inner child', which is most easily explained by relating to ourselves as newborn babies. We demand to be fed and nurtured, to grow both physically and emotionally, and this demand stays with us into adulthood. The outside responses to these demands are the pencil that draws the map of who we believe we are and how we relate to the world around us. The young child takes in information and, without the mature intelligence of an adult, stores this information deep in its subconscious mind. This information then forms our belief system.

For example, if we have not been allowed to express our feelings as children, especially anger and hurt, we will grow up into adults with an angry and hurt inner child. These repressed feelings, locked within our subconscious minds, directly influence how we relate and assess the world around us – almost as if we wore sunglasses all the time, never experiencing sunlight because the lenses filter it out. So the information we take in passes through a 'filter', and that can stop us from seeing things the way they really are.

Taking this further, it explains in simple terms why as adults we tend to repeat our unresolved childhood conflicts, making the same mistakes over and over again, and never seem to learn from them. So the inner child that has been 'wounded' becomes self-destructive and this can affect every area of our lives.

There are many ways our belief system can be damaged

but as there is no room to cover them all here, I am focusing on the areas my story highlights, but which are common to victims of abuse.

Co-dependence

We can become out of touch with our own feelings, needs and desires and end up relying on other people or objects to make us feel good. This is known as co-dependence and, as I am sure you will see, to some degree this manifests in most of us. The need for big houses or fast cars and the desire to feel that other people love and approve of us are fairly common. This relates directly to what happens to us in our childhood.

My dad had a drink problem, which made him into an unpleasant person quite a lot of the time. The effect this had on my family was that we spent a lot of time feeling anxious – there was always underlying tension in the house. Mum was perpetually telling us not to upset Dad because argumentative and controlling as he was, we never knew what mood he would be in. I remember being wary, sitting studying him and his body language, waiting for clues on how best to approach him. However hard we tried to take his lead, anxious not to upset him, wanting to avoid yet another argument, it never worked.

On the surface, we were a normal family, but in truth we were a family at war. As children we were always told not to tell anybody else our business, never to discuss with anybody what went on at home. This message was re-enforced in many different ways. Children learn by repetition. So, consequently, secrets became a big part of my life and very normal for me.

The way I used to watch my dad for clues to his mood, so that I could get it right and not upset him, I transferred onto Neil, especially at the beginning of our marriage. I blamed myself when things went wrong, and tried harder to please him, looking to him to make me feel good, because I was not in touch with my own identity. Co-dependence is characterized by the loss of our own identity and a dependence on others for how we feel.

Just as my parents had, Neil also constantly reinforced the need to keep secret what really went on in our family, which is why I felt unable to reach out to the outside world to rescue me from Neil's abuse.

Narcissistic Disorder

Again, when dealing with the hurt inner child, there is a common problem called 'Narcissistic Disorder'. When we are first born, we believe we are part of our mothers. Slowly, as we develop, we begin to recognize we are separate. During this development we need to be loved unconditionally and without judgement. If our parents for some reason or other are not in tune with this, then we are not reassured that we matter, that we can depend upon them. This can damage the child within, resulting in an adult who always craves love, attention and affection.

This behaviour becomes very apparent as the hurt inner child takes us on a quest for the perfect lover. Since no one is perfect, we then become disappointed with our partners and eventually sabotage our relationships. No matter how much love is available, it is never enough. Narcissistic Disorder can cause addictions and I have met many performers and athletes who suffer from a great thirst for continuous admiration and adulation.

My parents were neither physically nor verbally demonstrative of their love for me and as a child if I wanted a cuddle from either of them I had to instigate it myself. As a teenager I was looking for the perfect lover but continually being dissatisfied with one relationship after another. After Neil this need made me into a relationship addict and was the key motivation behind my single-minded desire to have a baby who I could love and who would in turn reciprocate that love. (Though my desire to have a baby was complicated by my grief over losing my first child and my need to expunge the guilt I felt for wanting to abort the foetus.)

Trust

One of the first issues we have to deal with as a developing child is trust. We learn how to trust our parents, then ourselves, and finally the outside world. If there are problems in trusting our parents, then beyond them the world becomes a dangerous and frightening place. One way of coping with this is to believe we will be safe if we can control everything. But this can become an addiction. In a relationship, a person unable to take control will either surrender it − miscalculating where to place their trust in their ingenuousness, becoming clinging and overvaluing the judgements of the person they are clinging to − or they will subconsciously retreat, becoming isolated, as though they had built a castle around themselves and pulled up the drawbridge so that no one can breach the walls.

Because I couldn't trust my parents I didn't trust myself or my own feelings and therefore believed that the world outside was a frightening place where people were out to get me.

At the beginning of my relationship with Neil I did

express doubts about his wish for a very quick wedding. But not trusting myself and my own feelings I was very easily overwhelmed by what I thought was a loving, caring, secure relationship. I unwittingly handed to Neil a lot of the control of my life at the time. You can see that I was gullible and naïve; I was oblivious to the fact that it was an intense, obsessive, misogynistic relationship, to put it in the mildest of terms.

My childhood home was often a very hostile place to be. The three adults were too busy arguing their case and had little time for the feelings or opinions of their children. Watching my father beat my brother Harry daily, after he got into trouble with the police, left me feeling angry, guilty, sad and powerless. I am aware that a witness to violence is also a victim of violence, and I couldn't talk to anyone about how I was feeling – there was no one to tell. In a similar way I was confused, humiliated, hurt and angry about my sexual abuse in the bike sheds at school but the shameful secret was locked up inside me.

I had no one to express my fear and sadness to and consequently was unable to resolve my unexpressed grief. As I searched for men and women to become my nurturing substitute parents, this further underpinned my relationship addiction.

Intimacy Dysfunctions

At this point in the analysis we hit another counselling term, 'Intimacy Dysfunctions'. The term 'intimate relationship' is used in this context to describe a relationship between two people that contains the components of unconditional love, and acceptance of each other for who they really are. This is an idealism we are all working towards.

As a child looks towards its parents, initially believing they are both perfect role models, it takes as a blue print the components of their relationship. When the child grows into an adult it then subconsciously transfers this blueprint onto future relationships.

One of the symptoms of an Intimacy Dysfunction which applied to me was that once a relationship got too close and literally 'too hot to handle' I would push my partner away by picking faults, criticizing and arguing. Then there would be a cooling-off period, followed by a passionate reconciliation until the relationship once again got too close. This pattern would be repeated over and over again.

The Authentic Self and the False Self

For me the dysfunctionality of the family raised difficulties in forming close relationships, with either boys or girls. Another problem arose in my parents' relationships with me. My father wanted to live his life through me. He was a clever man but was never given the opportunity to fulfil his potential; he would have liked me to be academic and do very well at school. On the other hand, my mother had totally different perceptions, more in keeping with the culture of the times. She felt I should leave school as soon as possible, go to work and bring money into the home, help her take care of my brothers and keep house. Like every child seeking its parents' approval, this caused great confusion in working out who I should be and who I really was.

When the parents push their expectations onto a child, over a period of time the child creates a false identity that grows with them throughout childhood. This is known as the false self. The child will come to believe it *is* that person, forgetting that the false self is really a script written by the parents. Their true identity is known as the authentic self. This causes problems when the child becomes an adult and tries to cope within relationships because they are then confused as to who they really are.

In my childhood, I was constantly criticized and humiliated by both my parents. I could not discuss the sexual abuse I suffered at school; indeed neither parent made any effort to give me any sex education. I was left with a negative sexual experience with no positive teaching to help me understand anything about sex. I thought that in any relationship with men the first thing I had to do was to offer my body. This along with the confusion of who I actually was is a more than adequate recipe for Intimacy Dysfunction.

In my relationship with Neil, subconsciously I tried very hard to re-create the relationship with my dad. I wanted Neil to give me the feeling of emotional security I never really felt with my father, unless I was being the person he wanted me to be. Without being consciously aware of it, I wanted to be loved, unconditionally, for the real Nikola, my authentic self. Before we married, I believed that was who Neil could see, that it was the real Nikola he had fallen in love with. How could he? By then I didn't even know myself who she was.

Emptiness

When we lose our true self, we lose control of our real feelings, needs and desires, and experience the feelings of the false self. We feel an emptiness, loneliness, a low-grade continuous depression. We are grieving for the authentic self we have left behind. Our wounded inner child feels empty and lonely, not really connected with life – our own life. I had these feelings after being sexually abused at school. At the time this happened there was little understanding that children could suffer from depression, let alone that sexual abuse could go on at school.

While I was married to Neil I contemplated suicide many times but not as a cry for help. As my days and nights ran into one long cycle of horror, unbearable pain and degradation, with no end in sight, it was the only way I believed I could escape.

Addictive/Compulsive Behaviour

During my relationship with Neil, the terror I was put through created a hormonal change stimulated by the brain, which produces adrenalin and noradrenalin. Although not seen as drugs these stress hormones have their addictive properties – hence the phrase 'adrenalin junkie', which is used to refer to those who e.g. take part in extreme sports. This addiction was manifest in my need to live dangerously and often take risks. I created angst and stress in my life to reproduce the fear state so that my brain would produce these stress hormones. The longer this continued, the more danger I had to have to create more stress and reproduce more fear in order to release those stress hormones so I could get my 'fix'. In my work as a therapist with adult survivors of all kinds of childhood abuse I have seen how common this pattern of behaviour is.

Although I haven't gone into details of it here, it is important to remember that the key factor in most addictions is the wounded inner child and its constant battle to be reassured and love and to have its needs met.

Magical Thinking – Romantic Love

In all children it's quite natural to think magically, but when children have been abused they never really grow up and continue to retain a child's magical thinking. One particular magical belief of mine was that if I could find the right man, marriage would make everything all right. Like most other teenagers I spent a lot of time fantasizing about relationships with pop stars. These fantasies would be about romantic love, rather than sexual love. This is how I felt about Neil at the beginning of our relationship – he was my knight in shining armour. I believed he had an intense desire to be with me and rescue the damsel in distress. This perspective of mine came from childhood and from reading many, many novels that were all based round this theme. Neil and I had very little knowledge of each other before we married and my feelings of romantic love never had any chance to mature into anything deeper. The reality of the relationship was that one very damaged person had recognized another damaged person. We were drawn together, resulting in a 'chemical reaction' between us that almost ended in death. Certainly by the end my personality had been chopped up like an onion and lay in pieces on the chopping board.

I have outlined in a very brief and simplistic way some of the most influential reasons why I and others like me can so easily fall victim to men like Neil. But why do victims of abuse stay with their abusers?

The Use of Fear in Domestic Violence

Fear is a very powerful emotion and can make it difficult for a woman in an abusive situation to see clearly what is happening, completely destroying what we would call rational thinking. Outsiders are often perplexed and ask the question, 'Why do you put up with it?' Some women are so confused that they don't even realize they *are* putting up with anything. Others will answer that it's because they love him. My answer as a young woman would have been, 'Because I am too frightened of what he will do to me if I left him.'

It caused great conflict within myself when I felt grateful to him for small acts of kindness – a reaction similar to what is known as the Stockholm Syndrome whereby a bond develops between captor and captive. When reality kicked in, I would feel as though I had betrayed myself.

In addition to the effect of fear, the abuser will have attempted to isolate their partner from all escape routes, cutting the ties to family and friends, undermining confidence, and completely disorientating them from the rational values of the outside world. Rather like it is for a long-term prisoner, the world beyond the victim's prison becomes a very frightening place. So, finding the courage to leave an abusive relationship, especially where children and financial difficulties add to the trauma, is extremely difficult.

Within the chemistry of a relationship the abusive partner recognizes the symptoms of a person who feels they are unlovable and begins to exploit and reinforce this vulnerability to gain control and cope with their own insecurities. Naturally, in the conscious, rational, logical part of our mind we know we are lovable, acceptable, okay people. In our subconscious, however, where all our memories, our habits, thought patterns and our core belief system are, we believe we are not. A belief will always override a thought, especially during times of stress and trauma. The repetition of our partner's continual undermining of our self-worth reinforces the repetition of childhood messages.

It is true to say we stay in an abusive relationship basically because we don't feel we deserve any better. This is it for us! I was being told daily that everything that happened to me was my fault, and Neil's constant repetition made me believe it too. Once I became free of him my beliefs became more rational and I started to question whether it really was my fault – and it wasn't all that long before I stopped colluding with my own abuse.

As you read my story you may have questioned why I never went to the police. There are various reasons for this. First, I was brought up to keep secret what went on in the family, and it was so ingrained in me that it stopped me telling anyone, even my parents, the full story. Also, at the time of my abuse – and even to the present day – my fear of Neil and what he will do to me is very real. This to many may be difficult to understand but that horrible feeling of fear, backed up with the violence and emotional abuse, is planted deep in my subconscious mind.

But the most important reason is that the events that take place behind closed doors are extremely difficult to prove. Neil's ability to completely manipulate the story to exonerate himself was crafted with the same skill as his systematic abuse. Even at the time it would have been very difficult to prove the whole horror of what happened; after so many years it would be impossible. The biggest fear for a lot of people who have been abused in any way is that they will not be believed. Their fear of being dismissed, or being misunderstood, is almost as bad as the crime itself. Here I would refer to Doctor Butcher's trivialized comments to me as I lay on the bed, visibly scarred by Neil's violence. His comments, from someone who should have known much better, took me right down into the bowels of hell.

Moving On – Dealing with the Cause not Just the Symptoms

Our healing has to begin at the cause of the damage, back in our childhood. If, as survivors, we can accept that and seek help to work with our wounded inner child to change our core belief system, then we can begin to turn our lives around. Take someone like me out of one abusive relationship and, without therapy, it will not take long for me to either find another abuser or go back to the original one. It is a vicious circle and as a society we need more resources to help prevent abuse in the first place as well as to help the victims.

I believe that to recover fully we have to work with trained and qualified psychologists, counsellors or curative hypnotherapists, but most of the effort must come from ourselves. The first step is to take responsibility for our own healing. Inner child work is extremely hard but also very rewarding and the most positive step we can take towards healing ourselves. If you feel you can make a start today do not procrastinate, but keep yourself safe if you are still in an abusive relationship. A list of organizations is given at the back of this book for when you feel you are ready.

Love Us or Hate Us but, Please, Don't Judge Us!

After reading this book, if you question any phrase, any action, any feeling as not being authentic, then you may understand why I have kept this secret to myself for almost forty years. When people continue to turn away from the truth because it's too scary and too painful or, like my story, too crude, they are letting me and others like me down. Neil and the many others like him will have won.

As a counsellor who has worked with victims of domestic violence, I am very well aware that this abuse will be happening to someone, somewhere, right now. Please stop saying things like: 'What is the point in trying to help these women when they keep going back?' 'They don't even want to help themselves, so why should we help them?'

'I think they have got a taste for it, they must be enjoying it.'

Let us look at the causes of the problems and actually hear what victims, who are actually survivors, are really saying. Listen to the music behind the words.

Writing this book has been therapeutic for me and with love and hope I reach out to all survivors of abuse.

I leave the last anguished cry from the young Nikola: 'Please God, help me, please somebody, anybody. Am I so awful and so bad that I deserve this? What have I done that's so terrible? Please, please, help me.'

If you want to know more about any of the issues in this book or would like advice on helping a person in a similar situation, please see the useful numbers below.

Rights of Women – http://www.rightsofwomen.org.uk
This site gives legal advice to women in England and Wales, all of which is free. They specialize on relationship breakdowns, sexual and domestic violence, among other legal issues affecting women.

The Samaritans – http://www.samaritans.org.uk; 08457 90 90 90
Use the website or call them anytime, day or night, they will offer a friendly ear and what you tell them will remain confidential.

**Refuge 24-Hour National Crisis Line –
http://www.refuge.org.uk; 08082 000247**
This free-phone number offers help for those living with domestic violence or those wanting to help a loved one in this situation.

BBC Hitting Home Campaign – http://www.bbc.co.uk/health/hh
Offers emotional and practical advice about how to cope with domestic violence.

Shelterline – http://www.shelter.org.uk; 0808 800 4444
Gives free advice on affordable housing throughout the country.

**National Domestic Violence Helpline –
http://www.womensaid.org.uk; 0808 2000 247**
Offering help and advice to the one in four women who suffer from domestic violence.

**Home Office – Domestic Violence –
http://www.homeoffice.gov.uk/crime-victims/reducing-crime/
domestic-violence/?version=1**
Domestic violence is a crime, this site details laws and gives further helplines.

Victim Support – http://www.victimsupport.org.uk; 0845 30 30 900
An independent charity giving help to victims throughtout the UK and Ireland.